Stay in His Grip,

Wanny Armstrong

Stay in His Grip!

Shane Stanton

The
HEART of a
GOLFER

The
HEART of a
GOLFER

Timeless Lessons and Truths about Faith, Life, and Golf

Wally Armstrong
with Frank Martin

GRAND RAPIDS, MICHIGAN 49530 USA

ZONDERVAN™

The Heart of a Golfer
Copyright © 2002 by Wally Armstrong and Frank Martin

Requests for information should be addressed to:
Zondervan, *Grand Rapids, Michigan 49530*

Library of Congress Cataloging-in-Publication Data

Armstrong, Wally.
    The heart of a golfer: timeless lessons and truths about faith, life, and
    golf / Wally Armstrong, with Frank Martin.
       p. cm.
    ISBN 0-310-24653-9
    1. Golfers — Religious life. 2. Golf — Religious aspects — Christianity.
I. Martin, Frank, 1958- II. Title.
BV4596.G64 A76 2002
242'.68 — dc21

                                          2002008990

This edition printed on acid-free paper.

All Scripture quotations, unless otherwise indicated, are taken from the *Holy Bible: New International Version*®. NIV®. Copyright © 1973, 1978, 1984 by International Bible Society. Used by permission of Zondervan. All rights reserved.

Published in association with the literary agency of Alive Communications, Inc., 7680 Goddard Street, Suite 200, Colorado Springs, CO 80920.

Interior design by Todd Sprague

Printed in the United States of America

02 03 04 05 06 / ❖ DC/ 10 9 8 7 6 5 4 3 2 1

CONTENTS

BEFORE YOU BEGIN

The great golf writer P. G. Wodehouse once said, "Golf, like measles, should be caught young, for if postponed to riper years, the results may be serious." I'm thankful that my heart was infected with the golf germ many years ago.

In one form or another I've spent most of my life around the game of games. I started playing and caddying at the age of eight, eventually carrying Gary Player's bags on tour. In 1968 I began playing and teaching golf professionally, and for twelve years I played on the PGA tour, competing against some of the best ball strikers in the world, including Jack Nicklaus, Arnold Palmer, Tom Watson, and many more. Since then much of my time has been spent teaching, speaking, and writing about golf, as well as conducting training clinics and seminars.

> THOSE WHO STRIVE TO TEACH MUST NEVER CEASE TO LEARN.
>
> —BILL STRAUSBAUGH

You would think that by now a man my age would have grown out of this obsession with chasing a tiny white ball around the fairways, trying to knock it into a small cup, but the truth is, I have a heart for the game today as much as I did the first time I stepped onto a golf course. More, in fact. My appreciation for golf has only grown, and because of it, I've been blessed with a wealth of life-changing experiences and relationships through the years.

I think the main reason I'm so fascinated with the game is that I love to learn. And no other sport provides more of an opportunity for growing in knowledge and skill and understanding. I have a passion for learning about golf and for sharing what I've learned with others, whether it's about the history of the game, stories about the players, or fundamentals about the golf swing. I've been that way for as long as I can remember, and I don't suspect that will ever change. I have the heart of a learner and a teacher.

During my graduate work at the University of Florida, I studied under a man named Conrad Rehling, who was a deeply spiritual professor and a nationally acclaimed golf instructor. Under his guidance, I spent a year and a half researching the human mind and how people learn, trying to discover all I could about how the brain processes information. I was fascinated by the topic and intent on finding new and creative ways to connect with people and help them understand basic concepts.

What I learned during that time is that, hands down, the most effective way to teach someone is through analogies and associations. Some people might call them word pictures. That's why I use a lot of training aids and mental comparisons in my clinics, always trying to show instead of tell. If a student is struggling to produce a circular swing pattern, I'll put a hula hoop around their body to help them get the feel of a true circle. If they are having a problem shifting their weight forward during the swing, we'll put the clubs away and spend some time throwing a football back and forth to help them sense how the movement should feel. Whatever it takes to divert their attention away from what they're doing wrong and onto what they need to be doing right.

I do this because it works. People tend to respond to mental images much more quickly than they would to a simple word of instruction. And once our mind's eye can conceive a particular swing thought or motion, the body is more likely to be able to achieve it.

Jesus used this same approach to impact the hearts of the people he taught, by using parables and word pictures. He made his teachings simple to understand by relaying them through stories and mental images. His example gives us great insight into how to best reach people with the gospel message and the truths of Scripture. God is still reaching out and teaching us through everyday experiences. He often engineers the events and circumstances of our lives to shape our hearts and help us grasp his will.

> FOR THE EYES OF THE LORD RANGE THROUGHOUT THE EARTH TO STRENGTHEN THOSE WHOSE HEARTS ARE FULLY COMMITTED TO HIM.
>
> —2 CHRONICLES 16:9

God understands that the lessons that really stick, the ones that truly shape our thoughts and values, are the ones learned through personal experience and example, trial and error. The hard-knocks school of learning. That's certainly been the case in my life. Through the years God has used events and people in my career to instill in me some deep and lasting truths about life and faith and myself.

There are times when God taught me more during one afternoon on the golf course than I could have learned from a year of Sunday morning sermons. There's something about the game that brings out the best and worst in all of us.

I've always thought of golf as an intensely spiritual sport—more so than any other game on earth. It's a game that is pure and uncomplicated, almost genius in its simplicity. Someone once said that eighteen holes of golf is a perfect microcosm of life on earth—a series of small decisions, each affecting the next. A few great shots and we feel invincible, on top of the world. Then one mis-hit later, we're knee-deep in the rough, wondering how we're ever going to recover. It's not uncommon during a three-hour round of golf for a person to experience every human emotion imaginable.

Like life, golf is a game that can never be mastered. A perfect round remains always in sight yet completely unreachable. And no matter how low we shoot, we can always strive to post one stroke lower.

I suppose that's another reason why I love the game so much. Day after day it brings me face-to-face with myself and my true character. I play to my strengths but still have to deal with my weaknesses. I step up to a shot I've practiced a hundred thousand times on the range yet still hit it left of the target. Some days I play well, and other days I completely stink up the course. Yet through it all I keep coming back, keep stepping up to the tee, keep working on my swing, always striving to play better today than I did yesterday.

PERHAPS THAT'S WHY I ENJOY GOLF: IT PUTS IN EIGHTEEN HOLES WHAT LIFE PUTS IN EIGHTY YEARS——UPS AND DOWNS AND A FEW GOOD BOUNCES.

——MAX LUCADO

The book you hold is my attempt to pass on some of the many lessons I've learned, lessons that have strengthened my heart both on and off the course. It's a collection of odds and ends, of stories and anecdotes from my years in golf, each used in some way by God to bring home a truth about life, faith, relationships, and my walk with Christ in general. They are but a few of the things I've learned on God's lesson tee. I share them with you not because I have any special insight or because I have mastered them, but because God has seen fit to share them with me and I now feel compelled to try to pass them on, just as I would any other bit of wisdom I might learn through my time on the course.

So do me a favor. If you are one of those with a heart for golf as well a heart for God, then grab your glove and your clubs and join me on the practice range. Let's see what lessons the Master has in store for us. If we pay close attention, maybe we can both shave a few strokes off our game.

FUNDAMENTALS

*The fundamental principles of golf break
down into: control, balance and timing.
All other things are merely incidentals.*
ERNEST JONES

*Confidence without ability is impossible to
maintain. You can't feel confident very long
if you don't know how to hit the ball.*
DOUG FORD

*The most successful way to play golf
is the easiest way.*
HARRY VARDON

1

Keep It Simple

If there is one common problem I see among amateur golfers and high-handicappers, it is that they tend to overanalyze the game—every aspect of it. They've read books and watched videos describing the "perfect" swing, and they desperately want to achieve it. They hold in their mind a detailed mental checklist of every movement necessary to hitting the ideal shot and go through that list before and during each swing. Without exception, this does little more than send them away confused and frustrated.

I see so many players approach the first tee with a sense of fear and anxiety. You can see it in their eyes. They look out over the vast array of green, lush grass in front of them, with traps and trees lining the fairway, and then their eyes focus on a tiny flag in the distance, barely visible to the naked eye. Three hundred and fifty yards lie between them and the hole, and they've got four shots to get it into the cup. The mere thought of it seems overwhelming to a frustrated golfer.

Almost without fail, the first-hole jitters get to these players. They swing too hard and slice the ball into the woods. Or they duff the club into the ground and send the ball trickling toward the cart path. Their second shot isn't much better, and once again they've set themselves up for another round of high scores and shattered expectations.

The truth is, golf doesn't have to be complicated to be played effectively. At its core, the game is really rather simple. You progress the ball forward with each shot until you get to the green, where you softly stroke the ball into the hole. It takes years of work and practice to shoot par, and no one expects the average golfer to do so. Bogie golf is a fine target for most weekend players and can easily be attained when we relax and keep it simple.

> I COULD HARP ON THIS SUBJECT FOR A LONG TIME, BECAUSE I AM THOROUGHLY CONVINCED THAT THOUSANDS OF GOLFERS TODAY HAVE HAD THEIR GAME HOPELESSLY RUINED BY NEGLECTING SIMPLE FIRST PRINCIPLES.
>
> —ANDRA KIRKALDY

Begin with the swing. Forget trying to find the perfect swing and work instead on creating the simplest one. Swing with ease and freedom. Practice letting the club flow in a simple, circular pattern around your body. The goal is to swing the clubhead in a circular arch around the body, letting the ball get caught in its path. Don't try—or expect—to hit the ball three hundred yards down the middle on your drive. Just focus on a smooth and complete swing that sends the ball toward the green with each shot. And don't worry about carrying the green in regulation. Most golfers are doing well to be within thirty yards of the target after two strokes, and there's no reason that even an average golfer shouldn't be able to get up and down from there in three strokes.

After a lesson with a student, I always encourage him or her to take the principles we've been working on to the first tee and to commit to them throughout the round. Most students find that if they'll just relax and take the game one shot at a time, what had seemed complicated and overwhelming is actually not that difficult.

CREATING A SIMPLE SWING PATTERN

Professional golf instructor Arnie Frankel wrote the following about the swing motion: "The ideal golf swing is a very relaxed motion. If you can just be relaxed, letting the clubhead go back and forward, on a plane like a pendulum, you will have the best effective swing.

"When I am hitting the ball at my best I feel like I'm gripping the club about as loosely as I possibly can. The club almost falls out of my hands. In practicing remember to practice small swings until the feeling comes back. Small swings until you can feel the clubhead swinging. Little to big is the way to go."

> DON'T HIT THE BALL.
> SWING AT IT. DEVELOP A NICE,
> GRACEFUL SWING.
>
> —BABE DIDRIKSON ZAHARIAS

Remember, when it comes to the golf swing, simple is always better.

SHARING YOUR FAITH

Most of us have at one time been given a project at work or school that seemed daunting. We wondered if and how we could ever get it accomplished. But as we began, taking it one step at a time, the task seemed to get easier by the day. We went from feeling overwhelmed to feeling confident. And once finished, we felt a sense of pride and accomplishment, ready to take on even a larger project.

This same principle holds true when trying to share our faith with others. For many new followers of Christ, or even for inexperienced veteran believers, the mere thought of sharing their faith causes their palms to sweat and their throats to constrict.

The first time I was asked to share my testimony about my relationship with Christ, I was terrified. Conrad Rehling, my professor and golf coach from the University of Florida, was a godly man and a committed follower of Christ. And when he discovered I was a believer, he asked me to go with him to a small country school out-side of Gainesville, Florida, where he had been asked to speak. I had not been a follower of Christ for very long and had little knowledge of the Bible, but Conrad somehow talked me into getting up and telling my story. "Simply open your mouth and God will give you the words to say," he told me. Then he shared with me from the Book of Exodus. Moses was being commissioned by God to bring the Israelites out of Egypt, and Moses was afraid he wouldn't know what to say. God told him, "I will help you speak and will teach you what to say" (Ex. 4:12).

> GOD WANTS TO USE YOU. HE HAS A PLACE FOR YOU, A PART FOR YOU TO PLAY, A SEED FOR YOU TO SOW, A CALL FOR YOU TO ANSWER. . . . LEADING PEOPLE TO CHRIST IS THE MOST JOYFUL EXPERIENCE I KNOW OF NEXT TO HAVING MET HIM MYSELF.
>
> —GREG LAURIE

As I stood in front of those two hundred kids, kindergarten through twelfth grade, I was petrified, but I did as Conrad suggested. I opened my mouth, and God took over. The words flowed. I simply told them how I had come to Christ and what he had done in my life. Ten minutes later I walked off the stage, not even remembering much of what I had said.

Speaking to the children that day was an invaluable experience for me, because it taught me that sharing your faith doesn't have to be difficult or complicated. The best and most effective approach is to keep it straight and simple, just like the golf swing.

When trying to lead people to Christ, telling your personal story is always the best place to start. It's real and authentic because it comes from the heart. And, most important, it's something almost everyone can relate to. When someone doesn't know Christ, they're seldom inter-ested in hearing about the Godhead Trinity or end-times theology.

What they want to know is why someone like you would choose to follow Jesus and make him Lord and Master of your life. They want to know what Jesus offered that you couldn't find anywhere else.

When you want to share your faith with someone and you feel overwhelmed, just remember the words of Jesus in Matthew 10:19–20: "Do not worry about what to say or how to say it. At that time you will be given what to say, for it will not be you speaking, but the Spirit of your Father speaking through you."

If you want to touch someone's heart, keep it simple. Tell them your story. Tell them about Jesus. It's not as frightening as you might think.

2

PLAY TO YOUR
STRENGTHS

I learned early in my career that my strength in golf was my short
game. I was a great putter and could get it close to the pin from
just about anywhere. Guys on the tour used to say that I could get
the ball up and down from a trash can. I really struggled with my
driver and long irons, and as a result was consistently scrambling to
get it close, but my short game always seemed to save me.

The main reason for this was my crazy swing. Ken Venturi, a
television commentator, used to call me "the dancer." I had a bad
habit of sliding my right foot back behind my left heel during the
downswing. At the top of the swing, my club shaft was pointed fifty
yards left of the hole, and to compensate I had to slide my hips forward during the downswing to get the club squarely on the ball. My
swing was atrocious, and it caused me to miss a lot of greens.

I remember playing against Tom Watson during the final round
of the 1977 Western Open in Chicago. Tom was as smooth as ever,
but I was all over the place. I couldn't hit a green if my life had

depended on it. I even sent one shot into the water and was forced to drop, but I was still able to get up and down for a par. I proved to be quite an escape artist that day; I finished one stroke behind Tom to take second in the tournament. It was a great feeling, but I went away wishing I could have done better—that my long game would cooperate.

> **A GOOD PUTTER IS A MATCH FOR ANYONE. A BAD PUTTER IS A MATCH FOR NO ONE.**
>
> —HARVEY PENICK

A professional I admired came up to me later and said, "Wally, you've got a million-dollar short game. If you could ever change your swing and hit more greens per round, you'd be able to win a lot of tournaments."

His comment lit a fire in my heart, and I began putting all of my efforts into fixing my swing, breaking down its flaws and working to overcome them. I spent hours on the driving range hitting ball after ball, focusing on keeping my clubhead straight at the top and planting my right foot firmly. After a while I could see a difference. My long irons started coming around, and I was hitting more fairways off the tee. So I continued working at it, month after month, teacher after teacher.

But in my exuberance to get better, I had neglected my short game, and suddenly I couldn't get it near the hole as often. My chipping and putting began to suffer. I was hitting more greens in regulation, and my scores should have improved, but they didn't. I was only scoring worse. My game continued to deteriorate over the next few years, until eventually I lost my place on the tour.

In my efforts to improve my weaknesses, I had neglected my strengths. I had forgotten that it was my short game that got me onto the tour, and I should never have taken it for granted. A player should always strive to improve the weak parts of their game, but never at the expense of their strengths.

It was a hard-won lesson for me—one that I will never forget.

CHASING A TIGER

Tiger Woods once tied Davis Love III at the Las Vegas Invitational, and the tournament went into a one-hole playoff. Love had the honors, and he nailed his drive 310 yards down the fairway—a great

> **KNOW YOUR STRENGTHS AND TAKE ADVANTAGE OF THEM.**
>
> —GREG NORMAN

length for most players, but easily beatable for Tiger. Tiger then surprised everyone by choosing to hit with a 3-wood off the tee. Just a few minutes earlier he had played the same hole with a driver, and his tee shot carried right down the center about 325 yards—an easy pitch into the hole.

Tiger surveyed the shot and then nailed the ball dead center; it came to rest just shy of Love's ball. This allowed Tiger to hit first, and he hit a perfect 9-iron to within eighteen feet of the cup. Love shot next, pulling an 8-iron into the back left bunker. Suddenly Tiger was in the A position. Love made a good attempt out of the sand, giving him a six-foot putt for a par, but he missed and came away with a bogey. Tiger two-putted for par and won the tournament.

When Tiger was asked about his club selection, he explained that he always likes to be hitting into the green first in match play, because if he gets a good shot it puts tremendous pressure on the other player. He knew not only how to play to his strengths but also how to put the opponent into a position of weakness.

And that's just one of the reasons why Tiger is the man to beat on tour.

KNOW YOUR SPIRITUAL STRENGTHS

Over the last twenty years I've developed a love for spending time alone with God, reading his Word, writing out my thoughts, and journaling my time in prayer and meditation.

I'm an early riser, usually waking before 5:00 A.M., so I've made a habit of giving the first part of my morning to the Lord. I read from

Scripture, as well as from a few devotional books I've run across. My favorite is *My Utmost for His Highest,* by Oswald Chambers. I read a short selection each day, meditate on his thoughts, and then spend some time writing out a few of my own. I've been through this book five times, yet I never fail to glean new insight and understanding from this amazing Christian classic.

> **THERE'S NO SUBSTITUTE FOR A DAILY AND WEEKLY WALK WITH GOD.**
>
> —BILLY GRAHAM

I would be lost without this facet of my Christian walk. I consider quiet times alone with the Lord to be my spiritual strength. It has proven to be the most effective and enjoyable aspect of my walk with God, and by remaining true to that commitment—by playing to my spiritual strength—I've found that it strengthens other parts of my life as well.

My advice to other believers is to find their spiritual strengths and build on them. Whatever gift God has given you, use it, perfect it, work on it regularly and consistently. Allow God to mold you to your purpose in his earthly kingdom.

DON'T NEGLECT QUIET TIMES

One last thought: Whatever your spiritual strength—whether it is teaching, evangelism, writing, giving, encouragement, leadership, prayer, or organization—don't forget to spend time alone with the Lord. Otherwise you'll feel as frustrated as a golfer who can consistently drive the ball 250 yards down the middle yet ends up three-putting every hole. Some parts of your game you just can't do without!

3

UNLEARNING
OLD HABITS

When Dr. Tom came to me looking for help with his swing, he was as frustrated as any golfer I'd ever seen. He'd been to teachers all over the U.S., trying desperately to improve the quality of his game, yet he couldn't seem to get past the wall he'd hit in his scoring. Tom was a psychiatrist who had done numerous studies on the left and right hemispheres of the brain. His specialty was analyzing how people learn, which made it that much more frustrating to him that he couldn't seem to figure out what he was doing wrong.

After our first lesson together, I could see Tom's dilemma. He had a hundred swing thoughts going through his mind every time he stood over the ball—keep your head down, left arm straight, eye on the ball, swing inside out, club on plane, pronate, supinate, take it back inside, shift your weight. It's a wonder he ever made contact. He was struggling with dozens of incorrect swing habits, each brought on by a preconceived notion about the proper swing pattern.

While visiting with Tom, I learned he had played baseball as a boy, so the first thing I did was put away his club and hand him a baseball bat. I had him hit a golf ball off a makeshift T-ball stick on the driving range. I wanted him to get the feel of how natural the swing can be when you don't think about it. It was amazing how long and straight he could hit a golf ball with a bat in his hand. Then I handed his club back to him and had him swing it just like a bat. He continued this motion, slowly moving the club down further, first at waist level, then even with his knees, and eventually at ground level. I teed one up and had him hit it, and imme-

> I AM CERTAIN THAT THERE CAN BE NO FREEDOM, AND NO NATURAL SWING IN HITTING THE GOLF BALL IF THE MIND IS OCCUPIED BY INSTRUCTING THE BODY.
>
> —J. H. TAYLOR

diately he was able to see and feel the difference. For the first time, he felt truly natural over the ball. He later told me his game improved overnight.

The key to learning in golf is that you must first see and feel what you want the club to do and then trust that motion in order for permanent change to occur.

MAKING THINGS TOO COMPLICATED

Like Tom, most golfers tend to make the swing much more complicated than it needs to be. They've heard and read so many tips on improving our game that their brains are on overload every time they pick up a club. What I did for Tom was help remove those thoughts and free him up to feel his way through the swing instead of thinking his way through it. I encouraged him to start over by taking him back to his days as a young boy, swinging the club for the very first time. Only then was he finally able to see the power and simplicity of a pure and uninhibited golf swing.

> FOR THE ADULT PUPIL OF SPORTS, IT IS NECESSARY TO HAVE AN UNDERSTANDING OF THE CHILD'S SUCCESSFUL APPROACH TO LEARNING, AND THEN TO ALLOW HIMSELF TO ADAPT THIS VERY SAME APPROACH.
>
> —VIVIEN SAUNDERS

Children come to the lesson tee with no preconceived ideas about how to play golf. That's one of the reasons I enjoy working with kids so much. There are no bad swing habits to break, no mental blocks to overcome—just a blank slate. Children are willing and able to learn.

Jesus loved teaching children for the same reason. He saw their childhood innocence as a trait to be admired, as a building block for true, Christlike character. In fact, he told his disciples, "Unless you change and become like little children, you will never enter the kingdom of heaven" (Matt. 18:3). In effect, he was telling them, "If you want to experience your true purpose in life, you have to start by unlearning old habits, by laying aside your misconceptions about God and trusting instead in his grace and forgiveness."

LEARNING LIKE A CHILD

In my life, I have never seen the truth of this concept better illustrated than in the case of my father. Dad was a self-made man who was strong, proud, and boisterous—a typical alcoholic. He was a stern disciplinarian, and I longed to be close to him, but he continued to push me away.

When I gave my life to Christ, the chasm between Dad and I grew even deeper and wider. Shortly after my decision, Mom gave her heart to Christ, and Dad became more defiant and angry than ever, calling us both weak and gullible. He couldn't accept our newfound faith in God. Mom and I tried to share our faith with him, but he had no interest in listening.

Several years before Dad died, he was in the hospital preparing for serious surgery. The doctors said we had a fifty-fifty chance of losing him. The thought that I might never see my father alive again weighed on my heart and spirit, and though I knew it was going to be tough, I had to talk to him about the Lord. I bent down beside his bed, and for the first time in our lives, we had a heart-to-heart talk. I tried to explain God's grace and forgiveness to him, to tell him what it means to be forgiven. I shared the essence of Ephesians 2:8–9 with him: "For it is by grace you have been saved, through faith—and this not from yourselves, it is the gift of God—not by works, so that no one can boast." Still, he couldn't seem to comprehend it.

"Wally, I'm not a bad person," he told me. "I've always tried to do my best to take care of Mom and the family." My heart sank. I knew he still didn't understand. As always, Dad was trusting in his own performance instead of God's forgiveness. Just as Tom had stood over the ball, frustrated

> IN LIFE, AS IN GOLF,
> MOST OFTEN THE OBVIOUS WAY IS
> THE INCORRECT WAY.
>
> —PERCY BOOMER

that he couldn't get his swing to work, Dad refused to let go of his preconceived ideas about God. Dad was convinced that if heaven did exist, the way to get there was to do the right things, to live a good life, to try to be honest, and then maybe God would accept you. The kind of love and forgiveness I was talking about seemed to be beyond Dad's comprehension.

Thankfully, God gave us several more years with Dad. During his recovery, he was forced to stop drinking and chain-smoking, and I could tell he was becoming more receptive. He began to read some of the Christian books I had given him, and for the first time in his life he read from the Bible. Dad began to change, and I saw a new man starting to emerge. We knew he might not have long to live, and we prayed daily that before he died Dad would accept Christ and his forgiveness.

Then one night, just a few months before his death, Dad called me into his room to talk. He told me that Mom and he had attended a Billy Graham crusade. Dad said to me humbly, "Billy said that when Christ enters your life, he takes the slate where he has been keeping a record of your sins and erases it. But not only that, he throws the slate away! Son, that's the kind of forgiveness I've needed."

I couldn't believe my ears. Dad had just explained the gospel to me! He went on to say that he had taken Mother's hand and had gone forward that night, giving his life to Christ by making a public confession of his faith. "Son," he said, "you don't have to worry about me anymore. I know where I'm going." It was one of the happiest days of my life.

Over the next few months, we watched Dad's health deteriorate, but his spirit soared. Every day brought a fresh discussion about his new faith. He was like a child again, learning and experiencing new and exciting things every day. The Bible tells us in 2 Corinthians 5:17, "If anyone is in Christ, he is a new creation; the old has gone, the new has come!"

THERE IS A WAY THAT SEEMS RIGHT TO A MAN, BUT IN THE END IT LEADS TO DEATH.

—PROVERBS 14:12

That's exactly what I saw happening with my dad. He began treating Mom and others with a kind of love and respect I'd never seen from him before. During Dad's last few months, he and I developed a closer relationship than we had had during my entire childhood. My only wish was that he could live longer, giving us more time to share in his newfound faith.

As Dad's health worsened, the doctors were forced to admit him to the intensive care unit of the hospital. Even though he was weak, he continued to share Christ with every person he came into contact with, from the doctors to the nurses to the fellow patients on his ward. He never tired of talking about Jesus.

One evening, just a few weeks before Dad went to be with the Lord, I could tell he was in a lot of pain, so I asked if he wanted me to pray for him. He shook his head and said, "I'd like to sing a song."

I was a bit taken aback, since I couldn't remember the last time I'd heard Dad sing. Then in a small, almost childlike voice, he began,

> *Jesus loves me this I know,*
> *For the Bible tells me so.*
> *Little ones to him belong,*
> *They are weak, but he is strong.*
> *Yes, Jesus loves me.*
> *Yes, Jesus loves me.*
> *Yes, Jesus loves me.*
> *The Bible tells me so.*

I wondered if this might be a song Dad once sang as a little child in Sunday school. I'll have to ask him the next time I see him.

4

KEEP YOUR
GRIPS DRY

As a professional golfer, there is no greater pressure than that of having to go through qualifying school to gain your credentials to play on tour. It has been this way for over thirty years. The school is held only once a year, and only a few select players make the cut.

My first attempt to qualify was in 1971, when I missed the cut by three strokes. In 1972 I found myself back at the Silverado Country Club in Napa, California, trying once again. If I earned my qualifying card, I'd be able to play on the PGA tour that year. If I failed, it meant another year of playing minor tours around the country.

During the final round of qualification, I found myself in great position. I'd posted some really good scores during the first three rounds,

DRY GRIPS MAKE FOR BETTER GOLF. HECK, BEN CRENSHAW LOST A CHANCE TO WIN A MASTERS BECAUSE HIS GRIP WAS WET AND IT SLIPPED IN HIS HANDS AS HE PLAYED A SHOT ON THE 72ND HOLE OF THE TOURNAMENT.

—DAVIS LOVE III

and all I needed was a decent finish to make the cut, somewhere around a 75 or a 76, I figured. I was sure I had it made.

Before the round I asked my caddy to wet the towel for me, assuming he knew I meant just a corner of it. On the second tee box I discovered that he'd soaked the entire towel. Storm clouds were brewing, and it was too late to go back for a dry towel, so I hoped against hope that the rains would pass us by. They didn't. By the eighth hole we were in a downpour, and I had no way to keep my grips dry. At Silverado the tenth tee is almost a mile from the clubhouse, so there was no way to get a dry towel at the turn. After the ninth hole I found myself in the shelter bathroom (outhouse, really), trying desperately to dry my grips with toilet paper. It wasn't one of my better ideas. I wouldn't advise that you try it—trust me on this.

My clubs were slipping and twisting every direction. With each shot, I searched in vain for another dry corner of my shirt, trying desperately to keep my hands in place, but everything was soaked to the bone. It was all I could do to hang on to the clubs, and my score was losing ground quickly. It took all the skill I could muster to make it to the green.

> MOST GOLFERS PREPARE FOR DISASTER. A GOOD GOLFER PREPARES FOR SUCCESS.
>
> —BOB TOSKI

Once there, I fought to keep my putterface straight enough to get the ball into the cup. By the seventeenth hole my grips were so slick that a 5-iron flew out of my hand and halfway down the fairway. It was one of the most frustrating rounds of my career.

Surprisingly, I was able to hang on well enough to post a 78 for the day, but that wasn't good enough. I missed the cut by two strokes and had to face another year of mini-tours before getting the chance to try again.

That year I learned a lesson that has stayed with me to this day: Never underestimate the importance of taking care of your equipment and be prepared for anything. Whether it's keeping your spikes clean, your gloves fresh and dry, your rain gear close at hand, your umbrella in your trunk, or a dry towel on your bag. You can spend years developing your skills, honing your swing, working on your short game, perfecting your putting stroke, but if your equipment isn't working, your game will fall apart. If you can't hang on to your clubs, your score is going to suffer—no matter how hard you've worked.

PREPARED FOR GOD'S SERVICE

There have been times when I've sensed the Lord feeling the same frustration with me that I felt that day on the course long ago. He takes hold of me by the grip, takes his stance, gets ready to make a shot, and suddenly I begin slipping out of his hands. Before the next shot he dries me off and makes another attempt, but once again I twist and turn and wriggle away, causing yet another duffed shot into the rough. Sometimes I even fly out of his hands entirely. In spite of his best attempts, my slippery grips continue to foil his plans for a solid shot. I can imagine his disappointment.

> THE BEST EQUIPMENT IN THE WORLD, USED IMPROPERLY, WON'T ELEVATE OUR GAME AN INCH.
>
> —JOHN FREEMAN

Thankfully, God is better at recovering than I am. In spite of my slick grips, he always seems to post the score he's after.

The apostle Paul encouraged Timothy to become "an instrument for noble purposes, made holy, useful to the Master and prepared to do any good work" (2 Tim. 2:21). That same advice is good for you and me.

As a follower of Christ, it's my job to stay ready for anything, to keep myself in top condition, and to remain yielded to his will rather than pursuing my own agenda. I have a role in God's golf bag, and when he needs me I should be ready, with a willing attitude and clean, dry grips—in essence, I must stay in his grip.

In real terms, staying in his grip means staying in his will and remaining disciplined, physically and spiritually. It means staying in prayer and continuing to seek God's wisdom and vision for my life. I need to understand my purpose within his greater plan—what kind of club I am in God's divine golf bag—and then allow myself to be refined for that unique and specific purpose. I must stay sharp, be prepared, and remain ready and willing. I must stay in God's grip, dry and usable, fit for service at all times. I must stand with the prophet Isaiah and say to the Lord, "Here am I. Send me!" (Isa. 6:8).

STAYING CLEAN AND SURE

Since that frustrating day in 1972 when I failed to qualify, I've learned a new ritual. Before teeing off the first green, I always check one last time to make sure I have a clean, dry towel handy. One missed cut was enough for me.

I also have another ritual. Every morning, before my feet hit the floor, I pray that God would guide me through the day, that he would check for any hidden flaws or blemishes that might hinder me from his true purpose for me, that he would help me stay pliable and ready for anything.

My goal as a believer is to always offer God a clean heart and a sure, dry grip and to remain prepared for his use, whatever and whenever that might be. The last thing I want is to be left in the bag during one of God's exciting and important rounds!

A DRY-GRIP TIP

Players will often find themselves on a wet course with more than one club in their hands before shooting. I notice a lot of golfers choosing the club they want, then dropping the others onto the wet ground. Try instead taking a few seconds to stick a tee into the ground and then place the handle of your club across the top of it, keeping the grip propped up in the air. It's quick and easy and will keep you from having to constantly dry off your clubs during play.

5

IMITATE YOUR
MENTOR

I n the 1940s Glenda Colette was known as one of the greatest
players of her day. She had a beautiful, effortless swing, almost
perfect in its execution. She was longer off the tee than most
women professionals and could finesse the ball better than anyone.
She won numerous tournaments in her career on the professional
women's tour.

In her book *Golf for Young Players,* written in 1926, Glenda
credits her swing to her instructor, a man named Alex Smith. Alex
was a great player in his own right—a man who had won numerous
tournaments—but he was known mostly for his near-perfect swing
and his penchant for teaching others.

At an early age Glenda would follow Alex around the course as
he uniquely demonstrated the many shots she might need during a
round. Instead of trying to break down her swing and analyze the
flaws, Alex would simply make the shot a few times and then have
her imitate his swing. She watched him make shots from every imaginable lie and distance, and then she would make the same shot,

keeping the image of his shot in her mind as she swung. She carried those images in her mind and used them throughout her outstanding career. Today her swing is still considered one of the best in the history of the game.

During the same years Glenda played on the women's circuit, there was another player on the men's tour getting a lot of press for his game. His name was McDonald Smith, and he was being discussed and written about as having the most perfect and complete swing the tour had ever seen. In fact, the great Harvey Penick once said, "The prettiest swing I ever saw belonged to McDonald Smith."

It's no surprise to learn that McDonald was Alex Smith's younger brother. Alex taught his younger brother the same way he taught Colette—through example. It's a good assumption that he did.

Imitation is not only the highest form of flattery; it is the best road to improvement.

Visualize the Swing You Want

As a child in Indianapolis, I never missed a chance to see the Indianapolis 500 Golf Tournament when it came to town each year. Several of the holes on the course were in the infield of the racetrack, and often during practice rounds the players could watch and hear the cars screaming around the track in preparation for a race. It was a strange experience, and an interesting place for a tournament.

During the tournament I'd scurry through the crowds to follow Gary Player or Arnold Palmer or one of my other heroes. I'd find a place along the ropes, as close as I could get, then watch their effortless swings and study their smooth and natural rhythm. I was amazed at how simple they made it seem. I imagined myself making the same flowing motion. Watching these professionals was always the highlight of my year. I never tired of crouching in the grass and peering across the fairway as the best players in the world went head-to-head with each other. It was during these times that I developed a passion and desire to make a career in golf.

Usually I'd be so pumped up after the tournament that I would rush over to my home course and play a quick eighteen holes before dark. Without fail, I noticed that my game was suddenly better, my swing more fluent and confident. By watching and studying these near-perfect swings, I was able to visualize and imitate them, integrating them into my own game.

> GENTLEMEN, WE ALL KNOW THAT YOU CAN'T BUILD UP A GOLF SWING STEP BY STEP. WE PLAY BY FEEL.
>
> —BOBBY JONES

I took that same principle with me years later as I played on the tour alongside many of the same people I'd been watching as a young man. Whenever I had a particularly unusual shot to make, I would role-play, trying to imagine a tour star who could easily pull it off. Then I would visualize myself doing the same thing and emulate their swing.

If I needed to make a long cut shot into the pin, I'd imagine watching Lee Trevino making the shot. I had played with him so many times that in my mind's eye I could easily see him cutting across the ball, almost in a slice pattern. Then I would visualize myself doing the same thing as I played the shot.

If I needed to carry one a long way down the fairway, I would imagine Freddie Couples as he brought the club way back past parallel, putting himself in a powerful wrist-set position to gain the greatest momentum and power. He was a master at this technique, and by imitating his rhythm and flow, I was usually able to pull it off, putting me in great position down the fairway.

The reason visualization works is that it helps us get past the technicalities of the swing and into the feel of it, the picture of it. Through visualizing the swing we want, we are better equipped to reproduce it.

Remember: If the mind can't conceive it, the body can't achieve it.

A Putting Insight

When I caddied for Gary Player as a college student, I was amazed by his accuracy with a putter. I used to stand back and watch him putt, and I noticed that he always kept his head perfectly still during his stroke. He once told me that on the short putts—anything inside of six feet—he made a habit of keeping his eyes fixed on the ground where the ball was sitting, even after he stroked it. Many players, he explained, let their eyes follow the ball to the hole, wanting to see the result. This often creates a tendency to mishit, as it causes the head to move slightly before impact. Our focus should be on watching the ball, not the line or the squaring of the clubface. Gary would keep his eyes straight down during the stroke and then listen for the ball to go into the cup. This allowed him not only to keep his head straight but also to see the line and angle of his clubface throughout the putting stroke.

> **THE SIMPLER I KEEP THINGS, THE BETTER I PLAY.**
>
> —NANCY LOPEZ

I implemented Gary's approach into my game, and more than anything I had ever tried, it helped me lower my shots on the green. Try it the next time you're on the practice green. Start by putting from about two feet, then work your way out to the six- and seven-foot range, keeping your eyes downward and listening for the ball to hit the cup. It's not as easy as you might think—at least in the beginning. It's hard to trust your line and keep your eyes fixed. But if you stay at it, you'll soon see the difference in your scores.

Imitators of Christ

Imagine what your golf game would look like if Gary Player or Arnold Palmer or Alex Smith or the legendary Ben Hogan could step inside of your body and play through you. What if they could flow their spirit through yours, pouring their skill and strength into your arms, legs, and mind, reproducing their perfect swing through your body? Your game would be taken to heights that you never dreamed or imagined!

Now imagine what your life would be like if Jesus stepped into your body and mind, flowing his perfect love and compassion and goodness into you—from his Spirit to yours. Would it make a difference in the way you treated people, the way you responded to situations, the order and direction of your day? Would it affect the daily flow of your walk in Christ?

> I PRAY THAT OUT OF HIS GLORIOUS RICHES HE MAY STRENGTHEN YOU WITH POWER THROUGH HIS SPIRIT IN YOUR INNER BEING, SO THAT CHRIST MAY DWELL IN YOUR HEARTS THROUGH FAITH.
>
> —EPHESIANS 3:16–17

As believers, we don't have to imagine that possibility. Jesus made that offer to anyone willing to trust and believe in him. Before going to the cross he promised to send his Holy Spirit to direct and empower his followers toward faith.

In John 16:13–14, Jesus says, "But when he, the Spirit of truth, comes, he will guide you into all truth. He will not speak on his own; he will speak only what he hears, and he will tell you what is yet to come. He will bring glory to me by taking from what is mine and making it known to you."

Jesus promised to impart a small piece of himself, a measure of his majesty and strength, into the hearts and lives of all who put their faith in him. Through his Spirit, we have access to the full measure of his wisdom and strength. The apostle Paul explained that through Jesus we are "able to do immeasurably more than all we ask or imagine, according to his power that is at work within us" (Eph. 3:20).

Christ offers us salvation, but more than that, he offers an empowering and personal relationship. When we give ourselves over to him, trusting him as our Lord and Savior, he comes to dwell within us—to impart his perfect strength and will into our lives.

Like Paul, you and I can come to the course of life and say with full confidence, "I can do everything through him who gives me strength" (Phil. 4:13).

How's that for a way to drop your handicap?

FROM IMITATOR TO EXAMPLE

In his letter to the Corinthian church, Paul said, "Therefore I urge you to imitate me" (1 Cor. 4:16). He had developed enough confidence in his faith to implore other followers to watch and learn from him, to allow him to be their example of a Christlike character.

St. Francis of Assisi understood this principle clearly when he said, "Share Christ at all times; when necessary, use words." That's a good attitude for each of us to develop—in both golf and life. When you see someone struggling with their game, show them a better swing. When you see someone struggling in their faith, step in and mentor by example.

PART 2

THE PRACTICE TEE

Always keep learning. It keeps you young.
PATTY BERG

*Don't be too anxious to see good results on
the scoreboard until you've fully absorbed the
principles of the golf swing on the practice tee.*
LOUISE SUGGS

*The correct follow through and finish indicates
that your swing has been one continuous
motion back and through. In other words, you
haven't paused to hit the ball. Rather the ball
is something you've "collected" in route to your
finish. Think of impact as nothing more than
a collision between the ball and the club.*
CRAIG SHANKLAND

The harder I practice, the luckier I get.
GARY PLAYER

6

HAVE A PRACTICE PLAN

On any given day you can take a trip to any one of the thousands of driving ranges across the country and see weekend golfers whacking buckets of balls. Take a few minutes to stand back and watch, and you'll begin to see why so many players struggle with their game. About nine out of ten players will be setting up ball after ball—usually with a

driver in their hand—and swinging out of their shoes as they try to see how far they can crush it. They'll go through more than a hundred balls in about twenty minutes, then pack up and head for their car, usually feeling pretty good about their practice.

Most of these players, however, will go to the course over the next few days and discover that their game is no better than it was. They'll struggle through the round, constantly chasing their ball into the woods and scrambling to get onto the green. Then they'll three- or four-putt. After eighteen holes they go home more frustrated than ever, making plans to get back to the driving range to whack even more balls, desperate to figure out why they can't seem to find their game.

The problem is not in the quantity of their practice but in the quality of it. Players like this usually have all the skill and determination they need; what they lack is a good, balanced practice plan.

It's important to remember that the true purpose of a practice tee is to prepare you for the game. Of course there are times when repetitiously hitting ball after ball is important—namely when you're trying to groove your swing. But beyond that, the range should be seen as a time to practice shots we might need during a round.

When I go to a driving range to practice, I begin by visualizing the course I'm going to play. I see the holes in my mind's eye, then I play through them one at a time. If the first hole is a long par-4 with traps down the right side, I'll pick a spot down the fairway on the left and aim for it. After a few shots I pick up the iron I'll need next and then aim at a flag on the range positioned at the same distance. When I feel good about that hole, I'll move on to the next. During a practice time I'll often go through an entire eighteen-hole course in my mind, and when I find myself standing on the first tee, I know exactly what I'm going to do, hole after hole. My practice plan has prepared me for the course.

> **EVERY TIME YOU GO OUT TO HIT A BAG OF BALLS, IT SHOULD BE FOR A DEFINITE PURPOSE.**
>
> DOW FINSTERWALD

The next time you're on the driving range, I encourage you to try this approach. Discipline yourself to take your time and practice one shot at a time. Don't rush through the shots, but instead practice with a purpose. In essence, learn to practice how you play. I think you'll be pleasantly surprised at the results.

A ROUND WITH DIRTY HARRY

I love playing in celebrity pro-ams, especially benefits, but they can often be nerve-racking. The crowds that come out to see celebrities play are usually bigger and louder than we PGA guys are used to (unless you're Jack or Arnie or Tiger).

Once I was playing at the Bing Crosby Pro-Am, and I found that my playing partner was Clint Eastwood—old Dirty Harry himself. We were to play three rounds together, and the first round was scheduled for the treacherous Cypress Point Golf Course at Pebble Beach. I knew immediately that I needed to prepare myself for a lot of distractions. To make things worse, I had inadvertently left my golf clubs at the airport and was forced to play with borrowed clubs.

The sixteenth hole at Cypress is one of the most famous and difficult par-3s in the world. It's a tiny green positioned 220 yards out over an inlet of the Pacific Ocean. The winds are constant and unpredictable, quickly changing with the tides. Often it's raining a bit on that corner of the course. The sea lions are barking, the otters are floating, and whales are spouting water everywhere. The distractions are endless, even on the best of days. But add to that mix the mob of people that would gather around the tee box to see their favorite celebrity—especially Dirty Harry—and you have an idea of what I had to look forward to that day.

> **THE ONLY WAY TO BUILD REALISTIC CONFIDENCE IN YOURSELF IS THROUGH PRACTICE.**
>
> SAM SNEAD

Knowing all of this, I went to the practice range before my round to prepare for my game—most specifically, the sixteenth hole. I teed up and hit several dozen 3-woods toward a pin 220 yards down the range, visualizing the hole in my mind. I imagined different scenarios and wind conditions, went through my pre-shot routine before each swing, and then hit the ball accordingly, firming up in my mind exactly what I was going to do once I stood at the sixteenth tee.

The crowds that day were even bigger than I had expected, and I was really struggling with my game. I was posting a decent score, but the course and the distractions were really wearing at my nerves. But when I teed it up on the sixteenth, the winds and conditions were just as I had imagined and practiced for. Suddenly my confidence began to soar. I had prepared for this very moment. I went through my pre-shot routine, stepped up to the ball, and hit one just as I had done in practice. The ball landed one foot from the hole—a tap-in for birdie.

I won't embarrass Clint by telling you how his shot went.

Practice is intended to prepare us for the realities of the course, but only the right kind of practice will do so.

DON'T BRAG TOO QUICKLY

That shot on the sixteenth green at Cypress Point was one of the best holes of my golfing career. I was pretty proud of it and loved telling the story. But God used it to teach me a lesson in humility.

The very next year I was standing on that same green with Vic Damone, my celebrity partner for the day. We were talking with astronaut Alan Shepherd, Jim Walters, and fellow PGA professional Jerry Pate. As we were waiting to tee off, I seized the opportunity to tell everyone, including the gallery, about my glorious shot of the previous year. I told them the story of how I had practiced and planned the shot ahead of time, then nailed my tee shot for a tap-in birdie. They listened intently until I finished, then Jim Walters casually looked at Jerry Pate and said, "Didn't you have a hole in one here last year?"

Jerry nodded and nonchalantly said, "Yeah."

Totally took the wind out of my sails. Especially when you consider that there had been only a handful of aces on that hole in the history of the old course.

"God opposes the proud but gives grace to the humble" (James 4:6).

SET REALISTIC EXPECTATIONS

One common trait I see among a lot of average weekend golfers is unrealistic expectations of their game. They often have full-time jobs and families to take care of, yet they want to play like the pros. Many of them could if they were willing to make the sacrifice, but I would never be the one to encourage them to do so. Families and careers should never be sacrificed for a game—any game. Only when someone chooses to make a career in golf should they begin putting in the time it takes to play really well, but even then they should carefully temper the time it takes away from their family, not to mention the time it takes away from their service to God.

> **IF YOU'RE SERIOUS ABOUT IMPROVING YOUR PLAY, BE BRUTALLY HONEST WITH YOURSELF.**
>
> GREG NORMAN

I tell average golfers to take a close look in the mirror and ask themselves some tough questions about their game: How much time do I really have to put into my game? Should I be spending the time practicing when I have other priorities in my life that are being neglected? And what are some realistic expectations of my scoring abilities based on the time I have to put into my game?

Once players discern the true potential of their game and honestly assess the amount of time they should be putting into it, they are equipped to put together the best practice plan to help them reach that goal. The key is a balanced practice that takes all of these factors into consideration. When you understand your limitations of skill, abilities, and time, you can better plan your practice, prioritizing your time on the driving range and the chipping and putting green accordingly.

When weekend golfers plan their practice, almost without exception they decide to spend much of their time on the range practicing their short game and putting—chipping around the green and getting in close to the pin. Nothing helps average golfers lower their scores more quickly than learning how to get up and down from around the green.

As I've often said to my students, "Unbridled expectations ruin many a pleasant round."

A SPIRITUAL PRACTICE PLAN

I often have the opportunity to talk to groups of men about their walk with the Lord. At every opportunity I encourage them to set aside the first part of their day for a time alone with God—praying, journaling, and meditating on Scripture. So often men come up to me afterward and confess the trouble they have staying committed to this routine. They begin a daily quiet time with good intentions but seldom follow through for more than a few weeks.

> I LIFT UP MY EYES TO THE HILLS—
> WHERE DOES MY HELP COME FROM?
> MY HELP COMES FROM THE LORD,
> THE MAKER OF HEAVEN AND EARTH.
>
> PSALM 121:1–2

The problem, I think, is that so many Christians don't understand the true purpose behind this regular time with the Lord. We've been told by pastors and other Christian leaders that it's important, so we trudge forward out of a sense of guilt or obligation and then wonder why it's so hard to stay on course day after day. But we should always beware of any plans that are based on our strengths rather than on our need for God.

It's much easier to stay committed to our quiet times when we understand their purpose. We should see them as a time of preparation for the course, to ready us for situations that may arise during the daily routine of living—something of a practice plan for life.

We all run across situations that catch us off guard. A boss asks us to do something unethical, a girl behind the counter throws us a flirtatious glance or phrase, a coworker takes credit for our work, our kids come home with the wrong kinds of friends, our accountant gets a little too creative with the tax forms. Life doesn't always give us a perfect lie in the rough, and when it doesn't, we need to be ready for the shot we need to make. If we've prepared ourselves ahead of time, these obstacles won't seem so frightening. We know what needs to be done because we've come to the course prepared for such a moment.

When we approach our daily quiet times the same way we approach the practice tee—with a specific and predetermined practice plan—it gives us a sense of purpose and direction. We're focused and in sync, with a specific goal in mind. We work with a healthy balance on both our strengths and our weaknesses.

> I'VE ALWAYS BELIEVED THAT SUCCESS IS ACHIEVED WHEN PROPER PREPARATION MEETS OPPORTUNITY.
>
> TOM LEHMAN

If we often struggle with a certain temptation to sin, this daily communion with the Lord is the perfect time to prepare for that weakness, to envision different scenarios where we might run across this temptation, and to determine ahead of time what our reaction will be when it does.

In any situation, it's our role to plan ahead, to pray and study diligently, and to ask God to give us the words and wisdom we need to tackle any circumstance or obstacle that life (or the enemy) may throw at us.

7

WORK ON
YOUR GRIP

Someone once said, "If you have a bad grip, you'll have a bad swing." That couldn't be more true. No matter how hard you work on your golf swing, without the right grip you'll never get the power or accuracy that you need.

The hands, through the medium of the golf club, are the only connection the player has to the ball. To make proper contact and to have the clubface aligned at impact, it's crucial that the hands be placed correctly on the grip. In effect, the hands must line up in perfect alliance with the clubface. This allows the hands and club to work together as one unit throughout the swing.

Many players grip the club as they would a baseball bat. This feels natural, but it doesn't work, because the strike pattern of the two swings are so dissimilar. In baseball we grip the bat in our palms and swing at an object above waist level. But when we take that grip to a golf club, it opens the face at impact, sending the ball slicing off to the right. Players with this type of palm grip typically dip down to strike the ball, causing them to lose solid contact.

In golf the grip of the club needs to be placed and held in the fingers of both hands. It's not a natural feel, but it's an important element to the proper grip. It allows the club to rotate just right under the centrifugal force of the downswing, giving it a much better chance of squaring at impact (assuming the proper swing plane, of course).

> **THE GRIP IS THE HEARTBEAT OF THE GOLF SWING.**
>
> BEN HOGAN

Poor hand placement usually starts when a player places the clubhead on the ground and then wraps his or her hands around the grip. This almost always moves the shaft into the palms, rather than the fingers.

The quickest remedy for this is to always start your grip with the clubhead above the hands, about eye level, and then place the grip gently into your fingers. Use the markings on your grip to make sure you've got your hands properly placed. When your grip feels sure, firm it a bit and then take the club to the ground behind the ball. Sam Snead used to say that the correct grip pressure should feel like you're holding a small bird in your hands—tight enough to keep him from flying away but not so strong as to crush him.

If you'll make this ritual part of your pre-shot routine, I guarantee that your grip—and your game—will improve.

PALM ALIGNMENT

Another important grip fundamental to keep in mind is that the palms of each hand must be facing each other. If they aren't, the hands will work against each other as the club is swung, twisting the face of the club and making solid contact with the ball virtually impossible. This unbalanced hand position keeps the wrists from making the correct setting motion on the way back and through the ball.

One good way to test the balance of your hands is to take a book and place it between your hands in mirror position, with your fingers spread slightly apart on each side. Hold the book toward the ground as if it were a golf club and then swing your arms around as if swinging a club. Your thumbs should be pointing upward at waist level. Now complete your swing to the top and then make a swing through an imaginary ball, watching your hands rotate on the downswing, squaring the book at impact, and then again bringing your thumbs to point upward in front of you and on through to the finish.

> **THE BASIC FACTOR IN ALL GOOD GOLF IS THE GRIP. GET IT RIGHT, AND ALL OTHER PROGRESS FOLLOWS.**
>
> TOMMY ARMOUR

Try this drill several times at home to get the feel of how the clubface rotation should work during a swing and how the hands work together to make this happen.

STAYING IN GOD'S GRIP

In golf, a proper grip aligns our hands with the clubface in a way that allows for the greatest power and control over the ball. Without a proper grip, there is no course on earth that we can master.

In life, it is prayer and communion with God that give us that same sense of authority, control, and direction. It is the one thing we need most to master the course of our life.

Prayer is our connection to God. It is the median that allows him to align our lives with his will and purpose. It is the one true link between God's heart and ours. Through prayer we acknowledge our need for God's forgiveness and presence in our lives. By laying before him our deepest yearnings, longings, and sins, we are allowing him full access to our lives, surrendering ourselves and our desires to his perfect will and direction.

The natural inclination of most followers is to try to live *for* Christ, rather than *in* Christ. We want to be *doing* something—moving, working, accomplishing. But through times of quiet prayer and reflection, we learn the importance of simply *being*, of lingering in his presence, of allowing him to be in control.

A golfer may know all the principles of the golf swing—backswing, downswing, hip turn—and he may read all kinds of books and articles about golf, but if his grip is not balanced and true, all of his efforts and knowledge about the game will be wasted.

LOOK TO THE LORD AND HIS STRENGTH; SEEK HIS FACE ALWAYS.

1 CHRONICLES 16:11

In the same way, as followers of Christ, we may know the Bible backward and forward and may be living for God to the best of our ability, but without the deep and personal communication of prayer, our lives will lack power and direction.

In golf, our hands must be alive to the clubhead. In life, our hearts should be alive to God's hands.

8

DEVELOP A PRE-
SHOT ROUTINE

If there is one obvious characteristic that separates professional
players from most amateurs, it is that pros, almost without exception, have a distinctive pre-shot routine they go through before each
shot. This is not an accident. Professionals have spent a lot of time
carefully crafting these pre-shot rituals to match their specific games
and personalities.

Golf is an extremely mental game. Just as the swing requires a
lot of physical habit formation, so also the mind must form its own
unique pattern and pace—sort of a mental groove.

When I was playing on tour I would often see players at a distance on another fairway. Though I was too far away to make out
their faces, I could tell who they were by their pre-shot rituals.

Jack Nicklaus used to stand behind the ball and glance back and
forth between the target and the ground in front of him. He was
picking out a small spot in the fairway about six or seven feet ahead
of the ball—perhaps a leaf or a divot or a blemish in the grass—that
was aligned perfectly between his ball and the target. This small spot

became his reference point, something to help him aim the club. After identifying his reference point, he would stand for a few seconds staring straight ahead toward the target. When asked about this ritual, he said he was "going to the movies." What he meant was he was actually imagining in his mind's eye watching himself play the shot, as if he were on a screen. He would visualize the flight path of the ball exactly as he wanted it to go.

Once he knew what he needed to do, he would take a few quick practice swings, step up to the ball, square his clubface toward his reference point in the fairway, and take the shot. More often than not, he would nail his target with pinpoint accuracy.

> **YOU WIN MAJOR TOURNAMENTS WITH YOUR MIND.**
>
> TIGER WOODS

They say that once during a tournament the television commentators had planted a microphone on Jack's collar in order to pick up his comments as he played. On one hole he had just stepped up to the ball to take his shot when a jet plane roared overhead and distracted him. He wisely stepped away from the ball, and as he did, the TV guys heard him say, somewhat under his breath, "That was a good one."

In his mind, he had already played the shot.

The late Payne Stewart, a friend and fellow believer, worked diligently with a sports psychologist named Dick Coop to develop an effective pre-shot routine. Dick would actually follow Payne around the course during a tournament and grade him—not on how well he scored, but on how consistently he stayed true to the ritual they had developed. Dick said that when Payne won the tournament at Hazelteen in Minnesota, in 1991, he scored above 90 percent in consistency. Throughout the tournament, his pre-shot routine didn't vary more than a second or two from shot to shot. He would go through his routine, commit to the shot, then execute it, and both Dick and Payne credit his success in that tournament to the confidence brought on by this steady pace and consistency.

Another friend of mine, Dr. Joe Clark, a PGA master teacher, has done a lot of research and study on the pre-shot routine, and for years he timed players with a stopwatch during tournaments to gauge their pre-shot patterns and rituals. Dr. Clark is from New Hampshire, and he spent many a snowy day watching tournaments on television with a stopwatch, keeping track of the players during their rounds. He was fascinated by the subject and spent years analyzing and studying this dynamic.

> THROUGH PREPARATION AND HARD WORK, YOU CAN PREPARE YOURSELF FOR A MENTAL ATTITUDE—A "ZONE." WHEN IT HAPPENS, ALL YOU SEE IS THE BALL AND THE HOLE.
>
> PAYNE STEWART

Dr. Clark remembers timing Greg Norman during all four rounds of the 1996 Masters. During the first three days of the tournament, he noticed that Greg had an amazing consistency to his rituals. From the time he took his club out of his bag to the second he struck the ball, twenty-six seconds would pass, varying no more than a second or two either way. Going into the final round, Greg led the tournament by seven strokes.

But something happened to Greg's rhythm during Sunday's final round. His pre-shot routines became longer and extremely sporadic, varying wildly in time and consistency. On one shot his ritual would last only ten seconds, and the next would take fifty seconds, then twenty, then forty-five. With each hole his score continued to slip, and the worse he played, the more sporadic his pre-shot rituals became. His pace—as well as his confidence—was shot. By the time Greg reached the eighteenth green, Nick Faldo had come from behind to overtake him and win the tournament.

Greg showed a lot of class that day, gracefully congratulating Nick on his win and biting his tongue before the cameras, but it must have been a grueling experience for him.

For the rest of us, it was a stark lesson on the importance of remaining calm and consistent throughout a round—of developing a good pre-shot routine and committing to it, no matter what.

PRACTICE YOUR RITUAL

The pre-shot ritual I've developed for my game is simple but effective. I begin by assessing the shot, gauging the yardage, wind conditions, and position of the pin and the obstacles around the green. Then I select the club I need and take a few seconds to visualize the flight pattern of the ball. I take one or two practice swings and then step up to the ball. I set the face, step into position—left foot first, then right look at the target one last time, take a short waggle, then make the shot.

This ritual may not sound like much, but it works well for me. And I've been playing long enough that I go through this ritual without even thinking about it. It's been mentally grooved into my game.

If you don't feel that you have a consistent or effective pre-shot routine, I encourage you to develop one the next time you're on the range. Don't make it too complicated—less is more. The key is to find something that feels comfortable and creates a sense of confidence within you. If you're a rather high-strung person by nature, a short routine would be best. If you like to take your time, then create a routine that allows you time to think and to slow down the pace a bit.

Whatever ritual you choose, remain true to it before each and every shot you take, whether you're on the practice range or on the course.

> GOLF, IN MY VIEW, IS THE MOST REWARDING OF ALL GAMES BECAUSE IT POSSESSES A VERY DEFINITE VALUE AS A MOLDER OR DEVELOPER OF CHARACTER. THE GOLFER VERY SOON IS MADE TO REALIZE THAT HIS MOST IMMEDIATE, AND PERHAPS MOST POTENT ADVERSARY IS HIMSELF.
>
> BOBBY JONES

CONFIDENT IN THE LORD

Just as doubt can cripple the mind of a golfer, it can also creep into the life and faith of a believer and diminish his effectiveness for Christ in the world. James 1:5–8 says, "If any of you lacks wisdom, he should ask God, who gives generously to all without finding fault, and it will be given to him. But when he asks, he must believe and not doubt, because he who doubts is like a wave of the sea, blown and tossed by the wind. That man should not think he will receive anything from the Lord; he is a double-minded man, unstable in all he does."

When we allow ourselves to question God's control and authority in our lives, it creates a sense of uncertainty and hesitation within us. We begin to doubt ourselves as well as God's ability to work through us in spite of our flaws and weaknesses. When that happens, we become unstable and unproductive and are often immobilized by fear.

But when we remain focused on God's strength and wisdom, it creates a sense of confidence within us, enabling us to pull off even the most difficult shots of life.

9

FIND A GOOD TEACHER

Someone once estimated that only about 5 percent of regular golfers have ever taken a golf lesson. In my opinion, this explains why so many players feel frustrated with their game and have so much trouble lowering their scores. Love of the game and good friends keeps bringing them back to the course, but much of their time there is spent in aggravation.

DON'T BE TOO PROUD TO TAKE LESSONS. I'M NOT.

JACK NICKLAUS

The problem with not taking lessons is that we have no way of seeing our swing from the vantage point of others. We can't see the small flaws that cause slices and hooks and other mis-hits, and our attempts at correction only create greater flaws. Most of us start out with poor fundamentals yet never take the time to learn the proper way to swing and play.

Any accomplished golfer will tell you that lessons from a good instructor are an integral part of a good golfing program. No matter how well you play, you can always get a little better, and the most effective route to doing this is through the advice of someone who really understands the fundamentals of the golf swing—someone who can see your swing from an outside vantage point.

Tiger Woods may be the best player in the history of golf. It's been said that he has more talent and natural ability than anyone ever to play the game. Still, Tiger regularly seeks the advice of Butch Harmon, his instructor. In 1997, after winning the Masters by an unbelievable twelve strokes, bringing Augusta to its knees and confirming once and for all that he was the best player in the world at the time, Tiger went home and called Butch to help him with his game!

Even more amazing, Tiger and Butch decided to change his swing pattern. Even though he could beat any player on the planet, Tiger knew that he still had some swing flaws that needed correcting, so he risked his career to make a change. It took him over eighteen months to groove new swing habits, and during that time many fans and sportscasters wondered about Tiger's "slump," but he stayed committed to the changes and has emerged today as an even better player.

> **WHAT YOU MIGHT LEARN IN SIX MONTHS OF PRACTICE, YOUR PRO CAN TELL YOU IN FIVE MINUTES.**
>
> JACK BURKE SR.

Wherever you are in your game, if you don't have a competent professional you go to regularly for help and advice, I encourage you to find one. Ask your friends and other players in your area for some referrals, then make the effort to select someone you feel good about—someone with a solid reputation for helping players improve.

In any endeavor, a wise person is one who is willing to seek and heed sound advice from others.

FIND THE RIGHT TEACHER

While looking for a good teacher, it's important to remember that not all golf instructors are the same. Though there are many competent teaching professionals at clubs around the country, methods and philosophies tend to vary pretty wildly. And just because a person works at a club and is a 1-handicapper doesn't necessarily mean he's a good teacher.

So ask around, interview several teachers, choose carefully, and don't sign any long-term agreements.

A TEACHING LEGEND

I wish I had known Harvey Penick. More than any man I know of, Penick has made an eternal impact on the game of golf—not through his playing, but through his wise and gentle instruction and his ability to pass on to others his simple but sound philosophies and his lifelong love of the game.

Harvey spent his entire career on the same course—the Austin Country Club. He began as an eight-year-old caddy and retired some sixty years later with the title of Head Professional Emeritus. But long after his retirement, well into his late eighties, he would drive his golf cart to the course four or five times a week to simply sit beneath the veranda of the clubhouse and watch players make the turn, surveying the beautiful rolling hills of Austin and dolling out sound advice to anyone who might happen by to solicit it.

Harvey coached players at every level of the game. Not only was he the primary instructor for a number of professionals on tour—Tom Kite, Ben Crenshaw, Mickey Wright, Betsy Rawls, Sandra Palmer, Terry Dill, and Don and Rik Massengale, just to name a few—but he also worked with kids, adult beginners, and frustrated high-handicappers. No matter where someone was in their game, Harvey was ready to help them lower their scores. And he always seemed to know just what they needed, both in their swing and in their mental processing of the game.

Tom Kite once said that during Harvey's years at the Austin Country Club, the club had a greater number of low-handicappers than any club he'd seen. Harvey's sound advice and instruction had made an impact on nearly every person that played the course.

But even more important than helping people lower their scores, Harvey had a way of imparting joy and delight to those he taught, passing on his love and passion for life as well as for golf. He was a deeply spiritual man who loved God and loved interacting with people.

"Some of my favorite memories," writes Tom Kite, "are the rainy winter days when no one was on the course and we could all gather around Harvey and try to get inside his mind. . . . The one thing that we all have learned from Harvey is love. A love of a game that teaches us more about ourselves than we sometimes care to know. And a love of the people that we share this game with."[1]

We should all strive to leave that kind of lasting legacy in the world.

THE ONLY TRUE COUNSELOR

I play a lot of golf with amateurs and high-handicappers during the course of my travels, usually during speaking and teaching events, and often I run across people who like to give advice to fellow players. A person will perceive a kink in their partner's swing and begin coaching them on ways to correct the problem. It always bothers me when I see this, because it does little more than add even more swing thoughts to an already overcrowded mind and usually messes up the rest of the player's game. The right time to fix a swing problem is on the practice range, not on the course. And one place you don't want to seek advice is from the hands of an unqualified amateur—especially one who may have as many flaws as you. If you want help with your game, look to someone who understands the fundamentals and intricacies of the swing.

Much more disturbing, however, are the many "experts" dishing out advice on how to live—not to mention the number of people

---

[1]Harvey Penick with Bud Shrake, *Harvey Penick's Little Red Book* (New York: Simon and Schuster, 1992), 11, 13.

willing to listen. Today, more than ever, bookshelves and airwaves are filled with self-help gurus, each claiming to have the secret to a better life, a more productive and happy future, and a more fulfilling existence. I'm sure most of these people are sincere in their beliefs, but I often wonder where their life philosophies come from—especially since so many of these philosophies contradict each other. What is the root and foundation beneath their advice?

> **PLANS FAIL FOR LACK OF COUNSEL, BUT WITH MANY ADVISERS THEY SUCCEED.**
>
> PROVERBS 15:22

When it comes to living a happy, successful, and rewarding life, why not look to the one who created it all—the one who understands us better than we can ever understand ourselves? It seems futile to spend our lives searching for meaning and significance among men, wondering who we are and what life is about, when the God who made us has given us all the answers we need.

God's Word is the only true foundation for life. It is our instruction manual, conceived and inspired by the author of all life and faith and wisdom, given to us as a guide to help us through any trial or problem we may ever encounter.

God also promised that if we put our trust and hope in him, he will never turn away and will always be there to guide us, even through the most confusing and frustrating times. The prophet Isaiah wrote, "Whether you turn to the right or to the left, your ears will hear a voice behind you, saying, 'This is the way; walk in it'" (Isa. 30:21).

We have at our fingertips the wisdom of the ages, the full measure of God's majesty, insight, and understanding, just waiting to be tapped—a counselor to help us when we need advice and direction.

Why would we ever look elsewhere when navigating the great course of life?

10

Practice Good Swing Mechanics

The golf swing, when performed correctly, is not a natural move. To groove an effective swing plane, a person has to learn to trust a concept that is foreign to the mind.

Logic would tell us that to get the ball on line, we need to aim at the pin during the swing, scooping the ball and bringing the shaft straight up toward the flag after impact. You can see this misconception at work in the minds of most beginners and high-handicappers as they try to muscle the ball forward.

But to get the most power and accuracy out of the swing, a player has to learn to trust the concept of allowing the club to orbit the body—letting the ball get in the way of the clubface as it circles the spine. When the swing is performed properly, the clubhead actually impacts the ball as the shaft moves from inside out, seemingly aimed somewhat right of the target at the moment of impact.

The player has to have faith that as the club meets the ball during this circular orbit, it will send the ball off in the right direction toward the hole. If you try to swing straight back and through the ball, pushing it toward the pin, it forces the clubface either to swipe across the ball, causing a slice, or to close at impact, creating a hook or curve. This, I believe, is why over 80 percent of golfers regularly slice the ball. In essence, the swing is something of a dichotomy. If a player tries to swing straight with the club, it actually causes the ball to curve. But if a player learns to swing in a circular, curved pattern, the ball will fly straight.

When I teach this principle, I hold a hula hoop around the student's body so that he or she can clearly see how the hands must work in a circle to let the club correctly orbit the body. I encourage students to visualize their arms swinging around their spine and body like a helicopter— their arms being the blades and the clubhead being the tip of the propeller.

> **THE GOOD PLAYER SWINGS THROUGH THE BALL WHILE THE AWKWARD PLAYER HITS AT IT.**
>
> KEN VENTURI

The focus is not on hitting the ball, but on creating the proper swing circle. Then as we carry this same swinging motion to the tee, the ball simply gets in the way as the club swings through its orbit.

I can never stress enough the importance of this simple principle. Before we can ever gain any power or accuracy in our game, we have to first allow this free-flowing, circular pattern to be grooved into our mind and body. Otherwise we'll spend most of our time on the course frustrated and confused.

A SIMPLE SWING THOUGHT

The main reason I like using a hula hoop to demonstrate the circular nature of the golf swing is that it boils the mechanics of the swing down to one basic thought process. There are many dynamics at work in the proper swing, and it is easy to get bogged down in the small details involved—the many things that happen before and during impact to create a good shot. But the swing is over within a fraction of a second, and no one can handle more than one thought during the process. So I boil it down to a simple mental image for the player to focus on.

The key is to practice this swing circle until it becomes ingrained in our body and mind, until it is second nature. Then we can take that swing to the course and trust what we have learned.

BEWARE OF GIMMICKS

I once played in a pro-am with a guy who had developed a popular training aid for golfers. I'd seen him all over television and in golf magazines, pitching this new product he had designed and created. All the commercials claimed this tool was guaranteed to help golfers develop better, longer, and more consistent drives every time. The trouble was, during the round this man only rarely hit a fairway. He spent most of the round digging the ball out of the trees.

As long as there are golfers, there will be golf gimmicks. But the only sure way to a better swing is through patience and practice. Learn the fundamentals of a proper swing and then work at it on the range—practicing those fundamentals and supporting them with the correct mental image.

PROPER PITCH SHOTS

One of the most difficult shots in golf is the short, high pitch shot over a bunker or water hazard. Most players struggle with this shot because it calls for a lot of finesse and timing with the club. It's hard enough to gauge the distance, but we also have to think about the height and flight of the ball, given the angle of the wedge.

The tendency during this type of shot is to try and scoop the ball with the clubface. We stand over the ball and see the steep face angle of the wedge, and we know we have to get it high, so we try to help the flight by hitting under the ball and trying to lift it into the air. This often creates a lot of wrist movement and mis-hits. It's a natural reaction on our part, but it kills the execution of the shot.

To create a proper pitch shot, we need to learn to hit through the ball and allow the club to do its work. In fact, the shot should actually feel as if we're trying to hit a low-flying shot with a steep-angled club.

A good practice drill for this shot is to take two sticks and some string and create a makeshift line about three feet above the ground in front of you. Then stand about six feet behind the line and try to hit balls underneath the rope with a wedge. Of course, you probably won't be able to do it. The angle of the wedge will send the ball over the rope each time. But by trying to keep it low, you'll be forced to hit through the ball, and you'll begin to feel the proper swing action for a good pitch shot. Once you get this feel, pick some spots out in the distance and practice hitting to them, using the proper stroke and motion. You should be able to feel the difference. And you'll find it's also easier to gauge the height and distance.

> GOLF WILL ALWAYS BE A TANGLE FOR THE AVERAGE GOLFER BECAUSE HIS SWING IS LARGELY A MATTER OF CONSCIOUS THOUGHT OR CONSCIOUS EFFORT, RATHER THAN THE BUILDING OF RIGHT HABITS WHICH OPERATE INSTINCTIVELY. THE GOLF SWING MUST FIRST BE LEARNED, AND THEN IT MUST BE FORGOTTEN, SO THAT IT CAN WORK IN A MECHANICAL WAY.
>
> GRANTLAND RICE

The single greatest thing you can do to lower your score is to increase your skills inside of a hundred yards. Work on your short game, and the rest will fall into place naturally.

THE MECHANICS OF SCRIPTURE STUDY

When I was a young Christian, someone told me one day that I needed to begin reading through the entire Bible. I felt really convicted by that challenge, so I began reading several chapters a day. I was intent on making it through the entire Bible within a year. My life was really busy back then, and several times I missed a few days and had to work feverishly to try and catch up with my self-imposed schedule.

Then one day someone asked me, "What did you learn this week during your studies?"

I thought for a moment and then answered, "I honestly don't remember."

That's when I decided I was going about it the wrong way. My heart was in the right place, but my plan was ineffective. I determined that I was still going to commit the first part of each day to the Lord, but I would do it by taking a small passage of Scripture and really digesting it. As I started to implement my new study plan, the Bible began to come alive for me. Often I would find myself spending an entire week on one passage, going over it each day and praying for God to speak to me through this small piece of truth.

> ALL SCRIPTURE IS GOD-BREATHED AND IS USEFUL FOR TEACHING, REBUKING, CORRECTING AND TRAINING IN RIGHTEOUSNESS, SO THAT THE MAN OF GOD MAY BE THOROUGHLY EQUIPPED FOR EVERY GOOD WORK.
>
> 2 TIMOTHY 3:16–17

Through this process I began to learn the power of God's Word and the many facets and dimensions behind each and every passage. As I read and meditated, it often felt as if I were trying to drink from a fire hydrant. The sheer depth and breadth and volume of God's Word is far beyond what any of us can possibly comprehend.

Once during the Kemper Open in Washington, D.C., I attended a tour Bible study, and the day's speaker was Doug Coe, a good friend of mine who works as an evangelist with a Washington-based ministry called The Fellowship. Doug is an incredible man of God who has reached thousands across the world for Christ with his ministry and friendship to others.

During his message, Doug made the statement, "It's not how much you get into the Bible, but how much of the Bible gets into you." Doug was reiterating the truth about God's Word that I had learned those many years ago. The most effective way to study is to take a small truth from Scripture and chew on it, meditate on it, allow it to sink into your heart and mind, and let God work on you through its message.

The prophet Jeremiah wrote, "When your words came, I ate them; they were my joy and my heart's delight, for I bear your name, O LORD God Almighty" (Jer. 15:16).

A change in heart or character comes when we allow God's Word to sink into us—when we let his Spirit transform us through the powerful truths of Scripture. That's how the Holy Spirit disciples us—one bite at a time.

Just as a golf club is designed to be swung in a circle around the body, you and I are designed to rotate our lives around God, for the purpose of fulfilling his perfect will.

OVERCOMING SWING FLAWS

Many people approach their golf game the same way they approach Scripture reading—by trying to absorb too much at once. I see golfers pouring over golf books and magazines, reading tip after tip after tip, trying to gobble it all up so they can improve their game. Or maybe they'll take a lesson and ask dozens of questions about what they need to do to play better. But they never take the time to absorb these principles, taking them one at a time and really working them into their swing. Instead of taking their swing flaws and trying to fix them properly—slowly, one at a time—they try to change everything at once. And in the end, all they've accomplished is even greater flaws and more confusion about their game.

A few years ago Tom Lehman and I reprinted a classic 1946 golf book by E. M. Prain titled *Live Hands*. In one section of the book, Prain was describing a round he had played with some businessmen, and he wrote, "In the course of one swing they were trying to do six or seven different things, but all that they achieved was an exaggeration of certain actions of that swing which deprived the whole rhythm. Their minds were focused on these motions instead of the ball at their feet. They had forgotten the first principle in golf, which is to hit the ball. Their play was unduly slow and they made a business of pleasure, while their game, far from improving, took a sharp turn for the worse."[2] The problem is a timeless one. Most of us have struggled with too many swing thoughts at one time or another. But it's much more practical and effective to take one good swing key and develop it, trust it, and work on it. You must allow it to become ingrained in your body and mind until it is second nature. When that swing key becomes part of your routine and habits, then it's time to move on to the next swing key. That's how you groove an effective golf swing.

It's also a good approach to developing an effective life in Christ.

---

[2]E. M. Prain, *Live Hands* (1946; reprint, San Francisco: Sports Log Publishers, 1994).

11

LEARN THE TRUTHS
BEHIND THE
PRINCIPLES

A friend once told me of his experiences with a series of golf lessons at his local club. He was a fairly new golfer who had never learned the proper swing fundamentals, and his game had a lot of flaws and inconsistencies.

During his first lesson the instructor had him take a few swings, then immediately set to work on changing his grip, as well as his posture and stance. "Now hit a few more balls," the instructor told him. My friend awkwardly swung the club, missing the ball altogether on his first try. After two or three more swings, the instructor again stopped him and began coaching him on the proper hip turn. He took my friend's club and demonstrated a few swings, then handed it back. "Now you try it," he said. My friend gave it a try, again somewhat awkwardly, and once more the instructor stopped him, this time to show him how to make a clean take-away.

This pattern went on for the entire lesson. Each time my friend swung the club, this instructor had another comment about some specific swing problem, usually unrelated to the previous one. "By the end of the lesson, I was more confused than ever," my friend told me. "My confidence was shattered, and I still had no idea what to do to fix my swing."

Sadly, this is not an uncommon experience for amateur golfers. Though there are many good golf instructors at clubs around the country, there are just as many who have no business teaching the game. They leave students frustrated and puzzled, wondering why they can't seem to improve.

As in any task, a good golf swing begins with an understanding of the basic principles—understanding the whys as well as the dos. It's not enough to know that we need to keep our head down, our right arm straight, our knees slightly bent, and so forth. We need to recognize *why* these things are important.

What are the underlying reasons behind these principles? Why does one grip work while another doesn't? What happens when the hands don't work together to rotate the clubface at impact? Why is the angle of the take-away so important to a good swing plane?

A CENTIPEDE WAS HAPPY QUITE,
UNTIL A TOAD IN FUN,
SAID, "PRAY WHICH LEG GOES
AFTER WHICH?"
THIS PUT HIS MIND IN SUCH A FIX,
HE FELL DISTRACTED IN A DITCH,
CONSIDERING HOW TO RUN.

ANONYMOUS GOLF JINGLE

I often tell my students that one ounce of whys is worth a hundred pounds of dos. Because when we understand the reasons behind the things we need to do, their truths become a reality to us and we become committed to them in real and definable terms. We see how everything works together to create a powerful swing and how each minute detail is important to the overall success of our game.

All the great golf instructors understand the importance of teaching a student the reasons behind the principles. In fact, they will tell you that a student who has learned all of the mechanics of a good swing without understanding the fundamental reasons behind them will almost always begin exaggerating the different components of the swing. They overswing at the top, their hip turn too pronounced and their follow-through overextended. And before long, these exaggerations have completely thrown off the good and natural parts of the student's swing, causing even greater flaws and inconsistencies.

This process of exaggeration is gradual, almost undetectable, but it is very real. Once a student begins focusing on *what* he needs to do without understanding *why* he needs to do it, he will continue doing and doing, until he inevitably ends up overdoing.

I encourage golfers to look for a good instructor to help with their game,

> THE BEGINNER SHOULD NEVER BE ALLOWED TO FORM BAD HABITS OR GET WHAT I CALL BALL-FRIGHT. IF YOU PUT A BALL DOWN TO HIM AT FIRST, HE WILL THINK ONLY ABOUT HITTING IT INSTEAD OF THINKING OF HOW HE SHOULD HIT IT. . . . BALL-FRIGHT HAS TAKEN HOLD OF HIM, AND YOU CAN FIND GOLFERS OF TWENTY YEARS' EXPERIENCE STILL AFRAID OF THE BALL. THEY NEVER KNOW WHAT A SHOT IS GOING TO BE LIKE TILL THEY SEE IT, AND TOO OFTEN IT IS NOT WORTH SEEING.
>
> ANDRA KIRKALDY

but don't allow your coach to lead you down dark alleys. When your instructor tries to change an element of your swing or posture, stop and ask, "Why?" When he relays a swing tip or a practice drill, ask, "What will this do for my game, and why does it work?"

A natural and effective swing begins with an intimate understanding of the underlying principles that make it work. Otherwise we'll always be caught blindly following the mechanics of the game with no real comprehension of the purpose behind them.

REASONS, NOT TIPS

The golfer is off his game—someone suggests that he try such and such a thing. It works like a charm, and the conclusion is that the tip effected a cure. In general terms this may be true, but not from the reason the golfer suspects. The tip may have given the golfer confidence, or it may have made him concentrate more, which is largely the same thing. The cure may have been what we loosely term a mental one, and although it works for a while, the old fault usually returns with a greater demoralizing effect. The last position is worse than the first, unless the golfer says, "Away with your tips, and show me your reasons."

—W. J. Thompson, *Common Sense Golf*

Practice Spiritual Discernment

When looking at our faith, we should apply this same practice of understanding the truths behind the principles. Before integrating a belief or command into our spiritual lives, we should ask ourselves, "Is this really a truth from Scripture, or just an interpretation? And if it is a mandate, what is the underlying reason behind it?"

Many Christians today are in the habit of blindly following the advice of their friends or pastors when it comes to understanding their faith. They accept the things they are being taught without ever questioning, without ever searching the Scriptures to test the validity of the messages they are receiving. They often assume the guidance they are receiving is accurate and true and blindly work to integrate those principles into their Christian walk.

But God expects more from his followers. The gospel writer Luke commended the Bereans for being of "noble character," because they "received the message with great eagerness and examined the Scriptures every day to see if what Paul said was true" (Acts 17:11). Even though Paul was known throughout the land as a great apostle of Jesus, the Berean Christians still recognized their responsibility to check out his words to see if they were scriptural and accurate.

But more than that, the Bereans wanted to understand the spirit of the message, as well as the letter of it. They knew that to truly drink in and digest the truths of God, they needed to have an intimate knowledge of the reasons behind the principles. They didn't settle for simply knowing *what* God wanted from them; they longed to understand *why* he wanted it.

That's the approach you and I should take. Instead of settling for knowledge about God and his Word, let's desire to understand his intent and purpose—his perfect and unchanging will.

To put a new twist on an old phrase, you might say that "one ounce of being is worth a hundred pounds of doing."

12

TRUST YOUR SWING

If you had a chance to watch Vijah Singh during the final day of the 2000 Masters tournament, you saw a touching exchange between Vijah and his young son on the eighteenth green, as Vijah nailed his last putt to win the green jacket. His boy had been following him around the course during the entire round, and the television cameras picked up the excitement in the boy's eyes as he jumped into his father's arms to congratulate him. It was hard to keep a dry eye.

Announcers had noticed that throughout the round Vijah's boy had been moving in close to whisper something to his father on just about every tee box. People began speculating on what he might be saying, until one official on the back nine overheard the young man say to his father, "Trust your swing, Dad." When asked about it at the press conference, Vijah said that he had been working to correct a specific swing flaw, and his son was reminding him not to get bogged down by negative swing thoughts as he played. At every opportunity his son told him simply to trust his swing.

One of the worst things you can do in golf is to lose confidence in your game during a round. And it happens more often than you might think—not only to amateurs but to seasoned players and professionals as well. I'm convinced that lack of trust is the single biggest cause behind poorly executed shots, for players at all levels of the game. When we stand over the ball and allow doubts to creep in—doubts about our abilities, our swing mechanics, the club we've selected, and so on—our

> **INSTEAD OF TRYING TO MANEUVER THE BALL WITH YOUR BODY, ARMS, AND HANDS, TRUST YOUR SWING AND THE CLUB YOU SELECT FOR THE SHOT.**
>
> BEN HOGAN

swing becomes forced and hesitant, which almost always leads to some form of mis-hit. I've seen it time and again, in other players and myself.

As an instructor, one common mistake I've witnessed is that players will come to me one day to help them with their game, we'll make some minor changes to their swing, and the next day they'll be out on the course playing eighteen holes. Almost without exception, this does more harm than good. Nothing frustrates golfers more than trying to work out a swing flaw in the middle of a round. It will mess up your mind, and your score.

The key is to learn to compartmentalize. When we're on the driving range, we can focus on the mechanics of the swing. That's the time to think about what we need to do to overcome a swing flaw and to work on changing the dynamics of our take-away or our downswing. And that's the proper place to spend hours working on these changes. But when we get to the course, it's time to put away these thoughts and play by feel. We need to trust what we've learned on the practice tee and let our swing flow freely—to let our minds be engaged in the shot making, not in the mechanics of the game. Too often players fall into the trap of playing what pros call "driving-range golf."

The fact is, a player has a better chance of scoring well with a poor swing and a lot of confidence than with the greatest mechanics in the world and a mind riddled with doubt.

FOCUS ON THE TARGET

The most common mental problem among amateur golfers is focusing on the ball instead of the target. I call this "ball fright." They stand over the ball and stare at it, with a thousand thoughts in their mind, each one letting even more doubts creep in. Oftentimes they seem mesmerized by this tiny white enemy on the ground before them. Instead of trusting their instincts and what they have practiced, they freeze over the ball. This usually causes them to swing *at* the ball, instead of *through* it.

One of the habits key to overcoming this problem is to focus on the target—on what we want the ball to do and where we want it to go—and then trust our swing to come through for us. We need to move through the ball with a free-flowing swing. In effect, we have to simply relax and let go and allow our instincts—what we know to be true—to take over. Our swing has worked for us before, and we should trust that it will again.

> IT REQUIRES HEROIC COURAGE TO TRUST IN THE LOVE OF GOD NO MATTER WHAT HAPPENS TO US.
>
> BRENNAN MANNING

Many people have a similar problem in life. When trials come our way, the temptation is to turn our attention to the problem at hand instead of trusting God to work things out. When we focus on a specific event or obstacle, it keeps us from seeing the bigger picture. We allow ourselves to freeze and tighten up, and we lose perspective. We get caught up agonizing over the crisis and lose sight of the target, and the longer we do this, the more doubts begin to creep in and shatter our confidence.

The key is to focus on the bigger picture, on allowing God to work through the problem to get us to a better place—closer to where we need to be. If we can simply take our minds off the specific trial or obstacle and instead look to the greater goal—the desired result—it frees our minds to relax and trust what we know to be true: God has always been faithful, and he will continue to be so.

God is greater than any trial that may come our way. It's our job to simply swing through the difficult times that come our way and trust him with the outcome.

EXPECT SOME TROUBLE

It's important to note that life, like golf, is a game of imperfection. We will never go through a round without finding ourselves in some sort of peril, without mis-hitting shots, without finding ourselves in trouble. Christ never promised us a worry-free round, but if we put our faith in him, he does guarantee a solid outcome. When we trust Christ with our future,

> YOU CAN TALK STRATEGY ALL YOU WANT, BUT WHAT REALLY MATTERS IS RESILIENCY.
>
> HALE IRWIN

we know that in spite of our imperfections, he will guide us closer to the target with each swing. Our triumph comes from knowing we have played the course in faith and obedience, focusing on the goal with each shot instead of on our own flaws and inconsistencies.

PART 3

COURSE MANAGEMENT

Success depends almost entirely on how effectively you learn to manage the game's two ultimate adversaries: the course and yourself.
JACK NICKLAUS

Golf is a thinking man's game. You can have all the shots in the bag, but if you don't know what to do with them, you've got troubles.
CHI CHI RODRIGUEZ

Lots of folks confuse bad management with destiny.
KEN HUBBARD

13

PLAY THE PERCENTAGES

I'll never forget how nervous I was prior to playing my first round in the Masters at Augusta. I was scheduled to tee off in the group between Arnold Palmer and Jack Nicklaus. It was in 1978, during the heyday of these two golf legends.

On the practice tee before the round I was hitting balls with Nicklaus to my left and Palmer to my right. I glanced up at the stands, and it looked like the parting of the red sea. Half the people were on one side, watching Jack, and the other half were watching Arnie, with no one in the middle. Talk about feeling out of place!

The first tee at Augusta is the most frightening shot a golfer can imagine—a huge, elevated tee box hovering high above a long, tiny fairway in the distance. Arnie was waiting to tee off, and I walked over to Jack and asked, "Do you have any advice for a rookie?"

He said, "You mean this is the first time you've played here? I thought you'd been here a number of times."

I was flattered to think that he saw me as a viable contender. Right away it put me in a positive state of mind. But I assured him that I had never played at Augusta. He then gave me this piece of advice: "In order to play Augusta, you really have to play to your strengths. You have to realize that there are a lot of birdies to be had out here. The par-5s are not too difficult, and you can usually get a birdie or an eagle if you don't waste your shots. But the most important thing to remember is this: Don't try shots unless you have a better than fifty-fifty chance of pulling them off. Otherwise the course will eat you alive."

> **FOCUS NOT ON THE COMMOTION AROUND YOU, BUT ON THE OPPORTUNITY AHEAD OF YOU.**
>
> ARNOLD PALMER

During the first round, it didn't take long to see what he was talking about. After birdying the first hole, I was flying high with my name at the top of the leader board. I got through the tough, short twelfth hole and then got blindsided.

During my practice rounds I had checked the course out pretty well. Every day, the creek in front and alongside the thirteenth hole was dry as a bone. On the last day of practice I went for the green in two on that hole and came up short, landing in the dry creek bed. When I got to the ball I saw that it was sitting up pretty nicely in the high grass, and I was able to get a club on it and get in close to the pin. Before moving on I took some time to throw a number of balls into the creek bed and practice hitting them. I discovered that more often than not, I was able to make good contact with the club, so I made a note to myself in my course journal: "Don't be afraid to go for the green." I knew that if I didn't make it, I had an 80 percent chance of having a decent enough lie to get up and down from the bottom of the dry creek bed. My strength has always been my green-side short game, and I'd rather be in high grass ten feet off the green than in the fairway for a sixty-yard pitch shot, which is usually my weakest short shot.

During the first round of the tournament I hit a pretty good tee shot on the thirteenth hole and had a long 2-iron into the green, so I went for it. I made decent contact but didn't quite get the distance I needed. The ball caught a bad bounce just in front of the fringe and went backward into the creek bed. I was a little disappointed, but I wasn't terribly worried, since I had suspected that might happen.

When I reached the green, however, my heart sank. It appeared that someone had put up some boards and stakes the night before, creating a small dam along the creek. During the night it had filled with water, and my ball had sunk into the middle of it.

> HOGAN WAS THE MASTER AT COURSE MANAGEMENT— USING ONE SHOT TO SET UP FOR THE NEXT . . . THE ULTIMATE CHESS PLAYER ON THE GOLF COURSE. . . . HE PLAYED ONE SHOT AT A TIME. THE HOLE HE WAS ON WAS JUST 1/18TH OF A ROUND.
>
> KEN VENTURI

In spite of that incident, I stayed committed to Nicklaus's advice and ended up finishing fifth in the tournament. At 8 under par, I came in only three strokes behind the winner, Gary Player, and beat "the Bear" himself by one shot!

The advice Jack gave me that day is good for all of us to remember. If you don't have a better than average chance of pulling off a shot, don't try it. Someday, if you keep practicing and playing, the shots that seem out of your comfort zone today will be routine iron plays. But until that time, be patient and play it smart.

TAKE THE SMART SHOT

In real terms, playing the percentages means knowing when it's time to lay up instead of letting it rip or going for the pin. There's not a golfer alive who hasn't struggled with the temptation to try and crush a 2-iron over the water to carry the green. We see the hole and we know that if we connect just perfectly, and the wind doesn't blow, we might just make it. But more often than not, such an attempt only leads to greater frustration as we pull another ball out of the bag and drop it along the water's edge. Experienced players know taking such a risk isn't worth the potential of a lost stroke, especially during a heated tournament.

Just yesterday I was watching Tiger Woods during the final round of the Williams Open. He came from behind to overtake Vijah Singh and win the tournament. Once again, Tiger showed why he is the number one ranked player in the world.

On one of the final holes, Tiger was faced with a long, tight par-4 and decided to lay up in the fairway, leaving himself a second shot of 188 yards. With his length off the tee, he could have chosen to take a driver or a 3-wood and try to crush it to within eighty or ninety yards of the green, but he didn't. The fairway was narrow, and he knew that all he needed was par to stay in the lead, so he didn't take any chances. He stayed calm and played the smart shot, and today he's got yet another win under his belt.

FLEE FROM TEMPTATION

As much as possible, I try to apply the principle of playing the smart shot to my life and faith, as well as to my golf game. I see no reason to take unnecessary chances where temptation is concerned. I know my weaknesses, just as you know yours, and I take every precaution to keep myself free from the temptation in those areas.

The enemy makes it his business to know our strengths and our vulnerabilities, and he preys on those areas that might cause us to fall. When we allow ourselves to be put into positions where he can play on our soft spots, we are doing nothing more than adding undo stress and complication to our walk with Christ. Even more important, we are letting Satan divert our attention from God's greater will and onto our own struggles and imperfections. Satan is a master at creating dams of temptation in our lives to keep us away from God's greater will.

As an example, I know many men have a problem with lust and sexual impurity yet continue to travel alone on business trips, knowing full well the temptations they will face in an empty hotel room far from home. These men are often committed followers of Christ who want to remain pure, yet the temptations of the road often prove greater than they can handle, so they fall to sin and afterward struggle with the pain and guilt caused by their indiscretions. This is sad, since there are simple and concrete things they could do to bypass these temptations.

For some men the solution might be as simple as calling the hotel before their trip and asking that the cable or in-room movies be blocked in their room. For others it may be necessary not to travel alone, perhaps making it a personal policy to always take a coworker or friend (of the same sex, obviously) or even their spouse with them. Whenever possible, they should try to stay in the home of friends or associates when they travel. The key is to know your weaknesses and do whatever it takes to give yourself the greatest chance of overcoming them.

> SO WHAT IS THE SOLUTION WHEN TEMPTATION RAGES? IF WE ARE WEAK AND HAVE NOT TAKEN PRECAUTIONS, IF WE HAVE NOT APPLIED PREVENTIVE MEDICINE, WE HAVE ALREADY FAILED. THE ONLY ANSWER IS TO PLAN, TO ANTICIPATE DANGER, TO PLOT THE WAY OF ESCAPE.
>
> JERRY B. JENKINS

When I traveled on tour, I made a regular habit of staying in the homes of Christian families along the road whenever possible. Sometimes they were friends; other times they were people who had heard of me through mutual acquaintances and offered to put me up. Some of my best experiences on tour came out of the many great times of fun and fellowship I shared with these wonderful believers. Not only did I make a lot of new friends along the way, but I was also able to strengthen my existing relationships as well. Through this simple practice, I was able to turn moments of potential temptation into times of great strength and edification.

If someone has a problem with alcohol, it only makes sense that he or she should stay away from bars and parties where liquor is being served. If a married person struggles with an attraction to a fellow coworker, a waitress at their favorite restaurant, or a person at their health club, it is their responsibility before God to steer clear of this temptation. This may mean finding another health club, discovering a new diner, changing positions at work, or even finding a new job altogether.

The point is, you and I know our weaknesses and our greatest points of temptation, and it is up to us to do whatever it takes to remain faithful to God in spite of them. We need to be able to plan our lives in the same way a successful golfer plans each hole, using our heads and not taking foolish chances.

Proverbs 16:9 says, "In his heart a man plans his course, but the LORD determines his steps." When we allow God to be our guide, he will help us avoid the pitfalls and temptations that surround us on every side.

14

STAY IN THE MOMENT

My first attempt at playing on the Senior tour came in 1995, at the Egypt Valley Country Club in Grand Rapids, Michigan. My game was really on at the time, and I shot an opening round of 67, to put me one stroke off of the lead.

During the first round, on the long par-5 seventeenth hole, my second shot came up short—about thirty feet off the green. I was setting up for a good pitch shot, hoping to get in close enough for a birdie. But before I hit the shot, my son, Scott, who was caddying for me, said "Knock it in, Dad!" Scott and I had been spending a lot of time practicing short pitch shots like this one during the practice rounds prior to the tournament, and he knew I could nail it if I got the right line.

I looked over at Scott and gave him a quick smile and a nod. He knew what that meant. I stood over the ball with one thought in my mind: Aim for the hole—dead center.

I hit a perfect chip that landed softly and rolled right into the cup for an eagle. After that I went to the eighteenth hole pumped and confident and came away from that one with a birdie.

On Saturday I was paired with Jimmy Powell, the leader of the tournament. For much of the round we were trading strokes back and forth. I'd take the lead, then he'd shoot a couple of birdies and pass me by. It was neck and neck. But somewhere around the ninth hole I began to lose my concentration. In my effort to pull ahead I strayed from my game plan and started to take unnecessary chances. I'd hit a poor shot, then walk up to the ball angry at myself, wondering why I couldn't relax and stay focused. I found myself standing over the ball with doubts creeping into my mind about my club selection or the angle at which I was coming into the green. I kept focusing on the trouble ahead instead of relaxing and trusting my swing. Hard as I tried, I couldn't seem to stay in the moment.

> **WHEN I THINK ABOUT THREE THINGS DURING MY SWING I'M PLAYING POORLY; WHEN I THINK ABOUT TWO THINGS, I HAVE A CHANCE TO SHOOT PAR; WHEN I THINK OF ONLY ONE THING I COULD WIN THE TOURNAMENT.**
>
> BOBBY JONES

I walked off the eighteenth green with a decent score for the day. On Sunday I shot a couple over par, but it was too little too late. Jimmy Powell, my playing partner on Saturday, went on to win the tournament, and I finished tied for twenty-third place—a respectable showing for someone new to the Senior tour, but not as good as I was capable of shooting.

Distractions will undo a golfer more quickly than anything else on the course. When we allow our mind to wander or to get ahead of us, our game is destined to suffer. Many a good round has been ruined by players who let their thoughts stray toward the next shot or the next hole or a looming bunker in the fairway ahead.

Successful golf demands to be played one shot at a time. In golf, each stroke must be taken as if it's the most important shot of our round. Whether we have a simple layup into the fairway or a ten-foot putt for birdie, it's crucial that we take great pains to analyze and plan the shot and then bring our entire focus into executing it well, because the success of the shot at hand will directly affect the lie and position of our next stroke.

When discussing course management, Arnold Palmer once said, "The key is playing the ball to the best position from which to play the next shot." No matter how difficult we try to make it, the essence of good golf can be boiled down to a basic strategy of planning each shot well and then executing the shot to the best of our ability, one stroke at a time. But to do that, we have to keep our minds free of distractions and negative thoughts. We have to stay in the moment.

STAY IN CONTROL

One of my favorite aspects of golf is that after every hole you get to start fresh. When you're standing on the tee box, you have the ball in your hand. No matter how poorly you shot the previous hole, at that moment you are in complete control. You can tee the ball up wherever you like behind the markers. You can choose how high or low you want your ball to sit up and the angle from which you want to come into the fairway. Every round of golf gives you eighteen different opportunities to take total control over your circumstances. It's a tremendous advantage in a game where course debris and unlucky lies can so easily add strokes to your game.

One of the most important strategies to good golf is to stand on each tee box and carefully plan how you're going to play the hole. Once you've hit your tee shot, the rest of the hole is governed by circumstances that are often out of your control. That's why it's so important to take advantage of your tee shot, while you are still in a position of strength and command.

Before teeing up, survey the course well. Plan exactly where you want to be hitting your second and third shot from, then decide which angle and club will put you in the best position to carry out that plan. Once you've purposed what you're going to do, put all other thoughts and doubts aside and commit to your plan. Play it just as you saw it in your mind's eye, one shot at a time.

FOCUS ON TODAY

When Bobby Jones was a young golfer in his teens, he had an opportunity to win a major tournament. Coming into the thirteenth, he was four holes ahead, with five holes to play. He was so sure he was going to win he started to let his mind drift and began thinking about what he was going to say during his acceptance speech when they presented him with the trophy. He made several crucial mistakes and ended up losing the tournament by one stroke. He later told a friend what he had learned through the ordeal: "Never shake hands with yourself until you have shaken hands with your opponent."

> **A SPIRITUAL LEGACY IS PASSING DOWN TO THE NEXT GENERATION WHAT MATTERS MOST. YOUR FAITH IN JESUS CHRIST AND THE CORE VALUES OF HIS ETERNAL KINGDOM.**
>
> STEVEN LAWSON

In golf and in life, it's never a good idea to get ahead of ourselves. The prize will come in due time to each of us, but today we need to focus on the task at hand—on staying in the moment.

LIVE EACH DAY FOR CHRIST

In Psalm 103:15–18, King David wrote: "As for man, his days are like grass, he flourishes like a flower of the field; the wind blows over it and it is gone, and its place remembers it no more. But from everlasting to everlasting the LORD's love is with those who fear him, and his righteousness with their children's children—with those who keep his covenant and remember to obey his precepts."

So often we spend our days in pursuit of fame or fortune or power, dreaming of the future and the glory that our efforts will bring us in the eyes of others. We long to be looked on with envy by our friends and peers, and we attempt to control our future through hard work and effort. But what the Lord wants is for us to focus on the here and now, on the task at hand, on making an impact in the world wherever we happen to be at the moment.

I remember a time toward the end of my PGA career when I was really frustrated with my game. I was hitting the ball well, but I couldn't seem to post the kind of scores I needed to stay in contention. Round after round I tried to make something happen, but I couldn't seem to pull it together.

Then one day I picked up a copy of a book titled *Burnout*. The book caught my eye because I really felt at the time that I was starting to burn out in my career. I don't remember much about the book, or even who wrote it, but I do recall the author's definition of life. He said, "Life is what happens to you while you're planning your future." That phrase hit close to home for me, because I felt I was stuck in that mode—always looking ahead and planning, trying to direct my life and career the way that I wanted it to go.

The realization of how I had been living made a big impact on me and proved to be something of a turning point in my career. I began learning to take one day at a time and to trust God more with my future.

St. Augustine once said, "We must care for our bodies as if we're going to live forever, but we must care for our souls as if we're going to die tomorrow." Another insightful writer had that same truth in mind when he wrote, "This life will soon be passed, only those things done through Christ will last." The only important and lasting impact of our lives will be what we have sown in God's kingdom—our love of the Lord and our willingness to keep his covenants and commands. And that's the only legacy that matters.

The charge for you and me is to stay in the moment, both in golf and in life.

15

PICK A TARGET, THEN PLAY THE SHOT

At the north course of the Los Angeles Golf Club there is a hole on the back nine that is a long par-4. You can't see the fairway from the tee box, but in the distance, almost 480 yards away, are three stately palm trees. They are no more than six feet apart from each other and sit directly behind the green.

I stood on that tee box once during a tournament and asked my caddy where I should aim. He said, "Aim right at those three trees in the distance, and it should put you right in the middle of the fairway." That was a good reference point for me. I took the shot and had a pretty good lie, right where he said I'd be.

But before leaving the tee box, my caddy told me a story he had heard about the late Ben Hogan. Hogan had stood on that same tee box years earlier and asked his caddy the same question. "Where should I aim?" He got the same answer that everyone gets—"Aim at the three trees in the distance." Hogan then turned to his caddy and asked, "Which one?" Now that's a man who knew how to focus!

That's why Ben Hogan has always been one of my favorite golfers. I once had the privilege of watching him practice at Shady Oaks Country Club, and his precision with a club never ceased to amaze me. Even in his later years he practiced every day, hitting shot after shot and striking his target with pinpoint accuracy each time. It was an awesome thing to witness.

I heard that Hogan was once asked about his favorite hole of all the courses on tour, and he named the eleventh hole at the Pinehurst number two course. His statement surprised a lot of people, because this particular hole doesn't seem very spectacular when you first come to it. I've played it a number of times, and it never struck me as a hole worth remembering. There are hundreds of holes on tour that make quite an impression on you, but this is not one of them.

> I'VE ALWAYS BELIEVED THAT SUCCESS IS ACHIEVED WHEN PROPER PREPARATION MEETS OPPORTUNITY.
>
> TOM LEHMAN

From the tee in this particular hole, the fairway appears to have very little definition. It's a long, flat hole that doglegs to the right, with small mounds and tufts of high grass on the horizon. All over the fairway are small bumps and swells and dips that you can't see from the tee box. In fact, you can't even see much of the fairway. It's like playing in an open hayfield somewhere in Nebraska. Yet as you walk the hole from tee to green, you discover that traps and troubles abound. And the green sits low in a small hollow in the distance, hidden from view. You can see only half the flagstick from your approach shot, and you have no idea where the cup might be located on the green.

At the time that Hogan played, there was even greater risk on the course; it didn't have precise yardage markers on every sprinkler head. Today's professionals have the advantage of knowing exact distances from anywhere on a course. They use yardage books mapped out by lasers to navigate around the course. But Hogan had to play by feel, trusting his skill and instincts to gauge the right distances.

Most players grieve at the thought of having to play holes like this one. They see the risks of getting into trouble and fear losing a stroke or two. But that's exactly why Hogan liked it so much. He knew that if he needed to gain a stroke on another player during the heat of a tournament, this was his opportunity to do so. He was so good at landing a shot exactly where he was aiming that he was able to stay out of problem areas. That's why his nickname was "the Hawk."

Skillful players welcome adversity. They see it as an opportunity to put into practice the talents they have honed through years of hard work and determination. And they view challenges not as foes, but as opportunities for growth.

Hogan's skill with a club gave him the confidence to face any obstacle head-on. He had spent so much time on the practice range learning how to stick a shot exactly where he was aiming that when potential trouble arose on the course, he had the faith to approach it with conviction and trust. That's why Ben Hogan is known as one of the greatest players in the history of the game.

ALWAYS HAVE A TARGET

I've noticed an interesting dynamic among golfers of all skill levels and handicaps. I'll be playing with a foursome and we'll come to a short

TAKE DEAD AIM.

HARVEY PENICK

hole with a very narrow fairway feeding toward the green. Often players will take an iron or a wood they feel confident with and land the ball pretty safely in the pocket. Someone will usually be five or ten feet into the high grass but still safely toward the target.

Then a few holes later we'll come to a long par-5 with water on the right and a wide, expansive fairway in front of us. Everyone grabs a driver and lets it rip. Almost without exception the balls will scatter all over the place, and usually at least one will end up in the water. We have a huge, forgiving fairway to work with, yet most of the shots will end up in some kind of trouble.

This happens because their focus is diminished. Their target is so big and wide that they let their guards down. They assume that they can stay out of trouble pretty easily, so they swing harder than usual, and by doing so they've set themselves up for another costly stroke.

Playing any shot or hole without a specific target in mind is a formula for trouble. Whether it is our tee shot, a layup in the fairway, or an iron into the green, it's important that we always know exactly where we want the ball to land, then aim for that spot.

I tell students on the driving range to work with each club to learn the exact distance they can strike with it, then to practice hitting a specific flag or mound in the range. I have them work at that shot until they can hit it eight out of ten times. Then I stress the importance of doing the same thing during a round. Before each shot, pick a spot in the fairway or on the green and then take all other thoughts out of your mind. Bring your entire focus on that spot, as if it were the flagstick. Gauge the distance carefully, pick the club you need, and then take the shot. More often than not, this practice will put you in great position to score well on every hole.

MAKE SURE YOU HAVE THE RIGHT TARGET

Back when I was a rookie on tour, there was a fellow rookie player who was also working to qualify for his tour card. On one occasion we came to Palm Springs after having been rained out in Hawaii. We got to California late Monday night, and the tournament was to start on Wednesday. We had one day to learn all four of the qualifying courses at Palm Springs. We couldn't possibly play all of the holes, and many of our caddies were kids from the area who didn't know the courses any better than we did.

During the first day of the tournament, this fellow rookie came to the third hole on a course he had not had time to survey beforehand.

It was a long par-5 with water running down the right side of the fairway. In order to have a good shot at the green, he decided to hit a 3-wood just short of the water. He hit a great shot, but it rolled farther than he expected and went right into the lake. It was a frustrating bit of bad luck, but the guy took it in stride. He figured he could drop and still get on with a solid shot, and maybe even land it close enough for a birdie. He hit a perfect 3-wood over the water and landed it safely on the green. It looked like he still had a chance to make birdie.

> **THAT'S WHAT PLAYING PROFESSIONAL GOLF IS ALL ABOUT, TO WORK HARD ENOUGH TO GET YOURSELF IN THE POSITION WHERE YOU MUST PULL OFF THE GREAT SHOTS IN ORDER TO WIN.**
>
> TOM KITE

But as he was making his way to the hole, he noticed another group walking up onto the green. He stopped and surveyed the landscape for a few seconds, then realized that he had been aiming at the wrong green all along.

It seems funny now, but that mistake cost this poor fellow some needed strokes. He hit some of the best shots of his career, only to find out in the end that he was aiming at the wrong target.

A lot of people make that same mistake in their lives. They spend their days working and planning and executing their game well. They try to the best of their ability to do everything right. They set goals for their family and their future, and they stay true to that vision. They even stop to reevaluate their purpose and direction from time to time. But when they reach the end of their lives, they look back to discover they had been playing toward the wrong target all along.

Christ is the one true goal that can bring meaning and purpose to your life. If your aim is not centered directly on his will and vision for your future, you are missing the only target that matters.

16

KNOW YOUR YARDAGES

Over the years I've played in hundreds of pro-ams, and I've noticed that most amateurs consistently come up short with their irons. Very seldom do amateur players hit their approach shots to the pin. They either come up short of the green altogether or they leave themselves a long putt to the hole.

In fact, the question I hear most often from amateur players in pro-ams is, "How do you always end up at the pin?" My answer is that I always take enough club. I know my yardages and I play to them. And if I have a question about which club to use, I almost always take the longer one.

I'm convinced most players struggle with their approach shots simply because they are underclubbing. They are using the iron they believe to have the right distance, but more often than not, it leaves them short of the target. This happens because most players don't make solid contact with the ball. The club they are using would be the perfect distance with the right swing and connection, but even a slight mis-hit will cause the shot to lose power and come up short.

In my clinics I explain that a ball struck squarely by a clubhead going 80 miles per hour will go further than a ball struck slightly off center at 120 miles per hour. Timing and control in the swing are more important than speed.

On the practice range, players usually hit balls farther than they do on the course. They are more relaxed and at ease, and their swings tend to be fluent and smooth. They tend to get spoiled on practice ranges, because each shot is hit from a perfect lie, and the range has no trees, lakes, or bunkers to get them into trouble. As a result, they swing easier and hit the sweet spot more often. But when they get on the course, their bodies tense and their swings become slightly more tight and rigid. This causes them to have less flexibility, which in turn slows down their clubhead speed. The result is their irons lose the distance they need.

> WHEN YOUR SHOT HAS TO CARRY OVER A WATER HAZARD, YOU CAN EITHER HIT ONE MORE CLUB OR TWO MORE BALLS.
>
> HENRY BEARD

I encourage players who struggle with this problem to simply take more club than they need with each approach shot. Eventually as they begin hitting the target more often, they will grow in confidence and their bodies will begin to relax, which will help them gain more accuracy. When this happens, they will find they carry over the pin on occasion. This is because they are hitting the sweet spot more consistently. With time they will need to start clubbing back down. But until that time, they should continue to use more club than they think they need.

In the words of Abe Mitchel, one of the greatest players and teachers from the early 1900s, "Never underclub is a good motto; or perhaps I should say, 'When in doubt, overclub.' The more you learn to play within yourself the better will your game be."

AIM HIGH

Another good tip I give to amateurs who have pretty good aim but always seem to come up short of the pin during their approach shots is to aim at the top of the flagstick. Most players aim just shy of the hole when they pitch in from around a hundred yards, hoping the ball will land on the green and roll toward the hole. They're often afraid of overshooting the pin, so their muscles tense and they come up short. Also, most players have a tendency to look at the cup when hitting toward it, and we naturally tend to aim where our eyes are focused. If players will aim at the top of the flagstick, they have a much better chance of landing one close.

Three years ago I was playing in the British Senior Player's Championship in London, and I found myself consistently coming up short when pitching from sixty to seventy yards out. I was really getting frustrated with myself. Then on the fifteenth hole, which is a long par-5, I hit a poor second shot and ended up seventy yards from the pin. As I stood assessing the shot, I decided I was not going to leave it short. I thought of the advice I had given so often to my students through the years—aim for the top of the flagstick—and realized I hadn't even been heeding my own counsel. I decided it was about time I took some of my own medicine, so I aimed for the top of the flagstick. The ball flew right into the hole for an eagle!

> IF YOU DON'T KNOW THE DISTANCES YOU HIT YOUR CLUBS——AND MOST GOLFERS DON'T——THEN YOU'RE GIVING AWAY A LOT OF SHOTS ON THE COURSE.
>
> GARY WIREN

It's easy to give advice. The hard part is learning to take it ourselves.

KNOW YOUR GAME

We've all been standing on a tee box of a long par-3 and heard one player ask another, "What club are you using?" His friend will say,

"I'm using a 7-iron." Then the one who asked the question will go to his bag, put away the club he has, and grab a 7-iron.

This is almost always a bad idea. Club choice in golf should be a very intentional and confident part of our game. Each player has his or her own unique swing speed and power, and we need to have enough consistency to know what club we should use for any given shot. To use a club that fits someone else's game is not only a mistake but a show of insecurity in ourselves and our abilities. It is the golfing equivalent of peer pressure.

The reason practice ranges are equipped with flags of varying lengths, each marked clearly, is so players can work with their clubs to learn how far each club carries the ball. Any good practice session will consist of a focused attempt to zero in and strengthen those distances until we have an intimate feel for our ability with each club in our bag. Then we can take that knowledge to the course and hit more greens and lower our scores.

WHAT KIND OF CLUB ARE YOU?

Here's a question you probably haven't considered: If you were a golf club in God's divine bag, what kind of club would you be?

Would you be a driver—a club used to move the ball a long way down the fairway toward his goal? Would you be a pitching wedge—an iron intended for accuracy around the green? Or maybe a putter—a closing club used to put the finishing touch on a specific hole or target?

When God has a task he needs to accomplish, he searches his bag for the right club for the job. He knows which irons he can depend on in a given situation. He knows which wedge will

> **BUT I HAVE RAISED YOU UP FOR THIS VERY PURPOSE, THAT I MIGHT SHOW YOU MY POWER AND THAT MY NAME MIGHT BE PROCLAIMED IN ALL THE EARTH.**
>
> EXODUS 9:16

get him in close to the pin. He knows the strengths and abilities of each and every club in his bag, and he'll use whatever he needs to accomplish his will.

He also knows which clubs have a history of letting him down, and these spend a lot of lonely hours in the bag—at least until they come around and begin to prove useful to him.

You and I have a unique and specific purpose in God's greater plan, and it's up to us to discover what that gift is and then allow him to use us at every opportunity. Whatever club God has created us to be, we should hope to fulfill that purpose with all our might and ability so that he can always depend on us to come through for him in a clutch.

It's also important to be content with the purpose God chooses to use us for. We are each designed with a specific intention in mind, and it isn't our job to question that role. I may wish I were a powerful 1-iron that can blast the ball 240 yards to the green, but if that isn't what I was made for, I would never be effective in that position.

Part of being a useful tool for Christ is knowing our purpose and then responding whenever and however we are needed.

17

EXPECT SOME BAD SHOTS

I remember playing a match once during college and watching one of the players in the group ahead of us. On the first hole he three-putted, then looked up into the sky with disgust. I wondered if he wasn't blaming God for his misses.

On the next hole he three-putted again and then proceeded to drop his club and put his hands on his hips in a fit of anger. Once more he raised his eyes upward toward the heavens. This time I could hear him shouting all the way from the tee box. He said three times in a row, "Get off my back!" That's when I realized he really was attributing his poor playing to some form of punishment from God. It was actually quite hilarious.

Though most players don't blame God when something goes wrong during a round, they do tend to expect too much from themselves, given the obstacles that abound throughout the course and the difficulty of the game.

At its core, golf is really a game of misses. The perfect round doesn't exist. The key isn't to play perfectly but to minimize the effects of your misses. The fewer mistakes you make, and the more good breaks you get, the lower your score.

Even the great Ben Hogan used to say that if he hit three or four really good shots exactly as he planned during a round, he was happy with his performance. It's interesting that so many golfers tend to complain if every shot doesn't come out the way we hoped.

Years ago I heard someone say that as a rule the average player will have five good breaks and five bad breaks during an eighteen-hole round of golf. It's known as the "five-and-five rule." I'm not sure who came up

> **THE TEST OF A GREAT GOLFER IS HIS ABILITY TO RECOVER FROM A BAD START.**
>
> P. G. WODEHOUSE

with it, but in my experience as a player and an instructor, I've witnessed its accuracy firsthand. At almost all levels of the game, players have experienced this principle. You get about as many good breaks as you do bad ones. It doesn't mean you will always have five of each. Some days you may have seven or nine bad breaks, other days you may have only two. And your score usually reflects the round's dynamics. But on average, the good and bad breaks tend to even out—five and five.

I tell players to take heart if they self-destruct on the first hole and come away with a double bogey. "Now you've got that out of the way, and you've got some good breaks coming," I say, though they don't always see it that way.

The key is to put the bad breaks behind you and focus on the future. Continue trying to put yourself in the best position to score, and your persistence will pay off in the end. The longer you play and the more accurate and confident your game becomes, the fewer mistakes you are likely to make. But even then, expect some bad shots during each and every round. Prepare for them. Even plan what you will do when they come. But above all, don't let them get you down or shatter your confidence.

What usually separates the great players from the average ones is their ability to deal with difficulties as they arise and to move through them to get in an even better position to succeed.

TENDER MERCIES

In 1978 during the last day of the Western Open at Butler National in Chicago, I found myself tied for the lead. I was in the last pairing with Tom Watson, who had dominated the tour that season. Coming into the fifteenth hole, we were dead even. The fifteenth is a long par-5 with a blind tee shot that feeds into a monstrous dogleg to the right. It was considered the hardest par-5 on tour at the time. On the left side of the fairway is an OB (out of bounds) fence, and the right side is nothing but trouble. Chicago was having a serious drought, and much of the fairway was flat hardpan. I knew that if I hit the ball down the middle, it would roll to the right and feed into a large thicket in the rough. The only place to hit was on the left side of the fairway just a few feet from the OB markers—a tight shot even for the best of players.

I hit a perfect drive—right where I was aiming—but halfway through its flight, a gust of wind caught the ball and drifted it right. I knew I was in trouble and dreaded the walk down the fairway to see where I had ended up. But as I came to the ball, I noticed it resting on the right side of the fairway on a severe slope, as if it were defying gravity. I couldn't imagine what was holding it up. For all practical purposes I should have been down deep into the bushes, but I wasn't.

Looking down at the ball, I couldn't believe my eyes. It had come to rest against a small chunk of melting ice laying in the fairway. The ground was hard and dry, and the heat was hovering above ninety-five degrees. I had no idea where the ice had come from.

I was smart enough to realize I had better shoot quickly, before the ice had time to melt, but I still had to wait for Watson and Dave

Eichelberger to hit. I quickly grabbed my club and positioned my shadow over the ball to keep the ice alive. I could literally see the ice melting as I waited. As soon as it was my turn, I cocked my club and took my shot, landing safely in the fairway just shy of the green. I think it was probably the fastest swing ever recorded on tour.

I looked up to the sky and said aloud, "Thank you, Lord. I needed that."

I didn't come away with a win that day—once again I came in second for the tournament—but I did learn a valuable lesson. Life and golf both come complete with enough bad luck and trouble to keep us all on our toes. Often it seems as though we

> I COMMIT TO A SHOT **100** PERCENT AND I DON'T WORRY ABOUT THE RESULT. WHAT THE BALL DOES AFTER IT LEAVES THE CLUBFACE IS BEYOND MY CONTROL, SO I ACCEPT THE OUTCOME.
>
> ANNIKA SORENSTAM

never get a break. But that's because we usually spend more time worrying about the problems we have than we do thanking God for the blessings he gives us each day. It's easy to dwell on the bad breaks, but let's not forget to remember the good ones—those small mercies that come our way when we least expect it and save us from the fate we really deserve.

DEALING WITH TRAGEDY

I'll never forget the fateful day my wife, Debbie, and I were traveling between Hilton Head and Greensboro for my next tournament. The kids were fast asleep in the back of the car as we moved through the long winding roads of the Carolina backcountry. There was a lull in our conversation, so Debbie reached over and turned on the radio. The first thing we heard was a news bulletin about a plane crash. Two jumbo jets had collided on the runway in the Canary Islands.

Debbie looked at me in horror and said, "That's my parents' flight." Though I tried to assure her the chances were slim that they had been involved, she seemed to sense otherwise. Something deep inside her heart told her that her parents were on one of those two planes.

Debbie's mother had recently been diagnosed with leukemia, and she wasn't expected to live much longer. So Debbie's father had booked a flight and a cruise, expecting it to be the last vacation he and his wife would take together.

Debbie and I had no idea what to do next. In our confusion we had lost all sense of order and direction. We had recently bought a condominium in our hometown of Orlando, and we considered heading back home until we could piece together more information about the accident. But then we thought of our good friends on the tour who would be waiting for us in Greensboro—friends like the Massengales, the Zarleys, and the Nelsons—the players and wives from our PGA tour chapel group. These friends had become like family to us through the years, and we knew they would be expecting us at the tournament. We also knew that if our worst fears were confirmed, we would rather hear about it among people we loved and cared for. We decided to go on to Greensboro.

For the better part of the day, our friends sat with us as we waited and watched for news about the plane crash. Finally, Debbie got a call from a family member, confirming that her parents had in fact been killed. It was one of the saddest moments of our lives.

Debbie and I will never forget the comfort we felt in the arms of these wonderful Christian friends. They cried with us, prayed with us, encouraged and strengthened us. God used them to help us get through this terrible tragedy in a very real way, and in the end, we emerged stronger and closer than before.

The psalmist wrote to the Lord, "May your unfailing love be my comfort, according to your promise to your servant. Let your compassion come to me that I may live, for your law is my delight" (Ps. 119:76–77).

In times of trouble, it's comforting to know we can turn to the Father of all compassion for help and guidance. We know that when we weep, God weeps with us. He engulfs us with his love and tenderness. And he works through those who are closest to us to wrap his caring arms around our pain and brush away our tears during times of sorrow and grief.

This side of heaven, life will always be riddled with trouble and strife. As long as there is evil and sin in the world, there will be hardship. But for those who follow Christ, the pain is fleeting and temporal. We know that if we just move through the hardship and press on, we will soon be in a better place.

> WHAT I LEARNED THROUGH MY BATTLE WITH CANCER IS MORE VALUABLE THAN WHAT I UNDERSTOOD ABOUT LIFE BEFORE I WAS HIT WITH ADVERSITY. I DO NOT SAY THIS LIGHTLY OR BOASTFULLY—I SAY THIS AS ONE WHO HAS BEEN HUMBLED BY PAIN AND UNCERTAINTY—I WOULD NOT BE THE MAN I AM TODAY IF I HAD NOT BEEN FORCED TO FIGHT CANCER.
>
> DAVE DRAVECKY

A SIMPLE PRAYER

After the accident, while Debbie and I were going through her parents' things, we found a small diary her father had started just a week before his death. In it he had written about how much he was grieving over the thought of losing his wife to cancer and how sad it was that this upcoming trip would probably be their last vacation together. He even wrote out a prayer expressing his grief over the thought of losing her, telling God that if she had to go, he wished there were some way he could go with her.

Somehow, finding that diary gave Debbie and I a great deal of peace and comfort. In a sense, we felt God had answered her father's prayer. Though we still missed them dearly, we knew they were still together, in a much better place.

TRUST IN GOD

The sovereignty of God,
*   count on it.*
The hand of God,
*   grab hold of it.*
The peace of God,
*   rest in it.*
The grace of God,
*   bask in it.*
The purpose of God,
*   seek to see it.*
The patience of God,
*   believe in it.*
The love of God,
*   experience it.*
The forgiveness of God,
*   trust in it.*

Wally Armstrong

18

STRIVE FOR PROGRESS, NOT PERFECTION

The late Ben Hogan used to tell of a recurring dream he had throughout his career in golf. In his dream he was in the middle of a perfect round, making birdies hole after hole, hitting each shot with pinpoint precision. He would walk off the seventeenth green having birdied every hole, elated at the possibility before him. But on the eighteenth green, each and every time he had this dream, he would miss a two-foot putt for birdie, blowing his chance for a perfect round. The dream always ended the same way—with Hogan walking off the green in anger and complete frustration.

Hogan spent his entire career in pursuit of the perfect round. Those who knew him said it was his obsession, his one and only goal. Though he was unmatched as a golfer, he never achieved his ambition.

The truth is, Hogan never played the perfect round because it can't be done. I'm convinced that even if Hogan had finished a game with a birdie on every hole, he would still go away unsatisfied. He would simply set his sights on finishing with an eagle on every hole. Who's to say that isn't the standard of perfection?

There's nothing inherently wrong with someone setting their sights so high that they are destined to be disappointed. Hogan did, and it made him the greatest player of his day. But in setting our sights so high, we are in serious danger of losing perspective on the game and on our lives. Striving to be the best you can be is a worthy goal, as long as you don't forget what's truly important.

> BEN HOGAN REFUSED TO BE SATISFIED WITH HIS GAME. THERE WAS NO SUCH THING AS GOOD ENOUGH IN HIS LANGUAGE. HE NEVER COULD BELIEVE THAT. THERE WAS ALWAYS SOMETHING ELSE THAT HE NEEDED TO DO.
>
> VALERIE HOGAN

The healthiest approach to golf is to strive for progress but not to expect perfection. Each time we walk up to a tee box, we should feel as if we know a little bit more about the game than we did on the previous hole. We should have a slightly better understanding of how to control the ball, how to trust our swing, how to keep our mind in the moment, how to ultimately lower our score. We need to seek the thrill of the process rather than agonize over perfection.

Golf can never be mastered, but it can be played well. And that should be our primary goal.

PRESSING ON

The healthiest approach to the Christian faith is to realize the futility of trying to live a perfect life—to come to grips with our humanity and our sinful nature—and to lay our struggles at the feet of Jesus. We are a fallen people, with flaws and imperfections running throughout our character. We will never be able to overcome our sinful nature on our own. Until we come to grips with that fact and accept the unconditional love and forgiveness of our Savior, we will spend our time in hopeless pursuit of perfection. And we will always come up short, no matter how close we come.

Jeremiah 9:23–24 says, "'Let not the wise man boast of his wisdom or the strong man boast of his strength or the rich man boast of his riches, but let him who boasts boast about this: that he understands and knows me, that I am the LORD, who exercises kindness, justice and righteousness on earth, for in these I delight,' declares the LORD."

True peace before God comes when we accept our failings and realize that God doesn't expect us to be perfect. He accepts us just as we are.

> **IF YOU COULD ELIMINATE THE OCCASIONAL BAD SHOT, YOU WOULD BE THE FIRST PERSON TO DO SO.**
>
> JOHN JACOBS

He knows we will never be sinless, but as we trust him, we will sin less.

A few years ago I was invited to teach and play golf in China with some businessmen from the United States. We found ourselves traveling together on a bus to the Shanghai Country Club. We rode for nearly two hours through the back roads outside of Shanghai to get to the course. My traveling partner was a man named Jim Hiskey, a good friend that I had known for many years and with whom I had a close, accountable relationship.

Because of my past, I'd always had a bad habit of looking down on myself and feeling that I wasn't good enough. I kept asking, "Why is it taking me so long to get better?" I always thought I should be trying harder. Jim had noticed this tendency and used this opportunity to confront me about it. He said, "Wally, you're never going to be perfect, but God doesn't expect you to be. He's more interested in the process of you drawing closer to him each day. That's all you should worry about. Do you know him a little bit better today than you did yesterday?"

His words really got my attention. I had spent so much of my life focusing on performance and trying to win the Lord's approval that I struggled constantly to understand and accept the unconditional love of God. Yet I knew in my heart that the only way I would ever be able to break free from the feelings of shame and inadequacy would be to simply let go and embrace God's forgiveness and love.

As in golf, the goal in life is not perfection, but progress. God understands our flaws and imperfections, and he accepts us in spite of them. The beauty of the gospel is that we are not expected to live a sin-free life. Jesus has done that for us, and through the miracle of the cross, he opened a doorway to God's kingdom for all who are willing to accept his forgiveness and his free gift of eternal life.

The apostle Paul wrote in his letter to the Philippians, "Not that I have already obtained all this, or have already been made perfect, but I press on to take hold of that for which Christ Jesus took hold of me. Brothers, I do not consider myself yet to have taken hold of it. But one thing I do: Forgetting what is behind and straining toward what is ahead, I press on toward the goal to win the prize for which God has called me heavenward in Christ Jesus" (Phil. 3:12–14).

The key to an effective walk with Christ is to put away our unrealistic expectations and our need to prove our worthiness and simply give ourselves over to his love and acceptance. When we do, it frees us to relax and live a life of joy and contentment, knowing that our eternal fate rests securely in the arms of Jesus.

Our goal before God should be to wake up each morning feeling a little bit closer to Jesus than we did the day before. To feel that we understand his will today slightly better than we did yesterday. To have a deeper love for his Word, a stronger commitment to his purpose, a greater appreciation for his sacrifice.

When we truly understand the magnitude of God's grace and forgiveness, it releases us to embrace his love and to enjoy our place before him.

I'm thankful that I had a friend like Jim, who loved me enough to confront me when he saw my self-destructive habits and tendencies. God used him to bring me face-to-face with my serious lack of trust and faith. Through that experience, I've been able to open up and let God love me just as I am.

I hope you have friends like Jim in your life. And I hope you can be that kind of friend to others.

19

TRUST YOUR SKILLS,
NOT YOUR INSTINCTS

Some of my favorite memories from my days on the tour came from the numerous practice rounds I got to play with Gary Player. As a young golfer, I had the privilege of caddying for Gary, and after earning my card to play on the tour, our friendship continued to grow. Only now I was competing against him, instead of with him.

Whenever possible, Gary and I would hook up to play practice rounds together before a tournament. Looking back, I think I learned more about the game during those rounds than I did at any other time in my career.

Often we would take close to three or four hours to play only nine holes. We'd hit several balls off of the tee, then walk around the greens dropping balls all over the place, practicing every imaginable shot. We'd practice hitting out of the sand, off of the hardpan, out of the thick rough, under low-hanging limbs, over trees and obstacles. We would even drop behind trees to see if we could figure out the best way to recover. Gary and I would compete to see who could pull off the best shot from different situations. Often our caddies would sit in a shady spot along the green and watch as the balls came soaring in.

When we were on the green, Gary used to challenge his faithful caddy, Rabbit, to try and stump him. Rabbit loved every minute of it. "Give me a shot I can't pull off," Gary would say. Rabbit would find a spot around the green and bury the ball deep in the high grass or on the high lip of a deep bunker, but inevitably Gary would be able to get it up and down. Nothing gave him more of a thrill than pulling off a seemingly impossible shot.

> THERE ARE NO BORN GOLFERS.
> SOME HAVE MORE NATURAL ABILITY
> THAN OTHERS, BUT THEY'VE
> ALL BEEN MADE.
>
> BEN HOGAN

One of the reasons Gary was such a powerful player is that he knew how to practice. He never wanted to come to a shot during a game that he hadn't hit before. He practiced every conceivable shot and hazard he might run into during a tournament. And because of this, he was able to play with greater confidence than any player I have ever known. I've never once seen Gary come to a shot that he didn't know how to hit. No matter how bad the lie or trouble, he always seemed to know what to do, and he knew he could do it! With Gary, there was never any guesswork. He had every imaginable shot in his bag.

Because of Gary's influence, I caught his spirit and integrated his practice habits into my own game. One of my greatest strengths as a player has always been that I can get up and down from just about anywhere on the course, and I attribute that reputation to my many practice rounds with Gary. I learned from him how to sharpen my skills as a player, and it created a confidence in my game and my abilities that I could have never attained otherwise.

That confidence is something I could never have developed on the driving range. Though there are times when it's important to work on a specific problem or flaw on the range, real growth comes through on-the-job training—through learning how to manage the real-life obstacles that are bound to come during each and every round.

The tendencies for most golfers is to think that if they hit enough balls on the range, usually from perfect lies, their instincts will get them through the problems on the course. Sometimes they do. But more often than not, it is skill and confidence that come through for us in a pinch—knowing we can pull off a shot because we've done it before.

Growth through Hardship

Several times during one of my many practice rounds with Gary Player, I came to a difficult lie and asked him, "Show me how you would make this shot." Often he would give me pointers and then demonstrate how he would do it. But then he would say to me, "You really need to experiment and learn what works best for you. I'll give you advice when I can, but if you want to really learn how to play, learn to play your own game."

> You build a golf game like you build a wall, one brick at a time
>
> TONY LEMA

Gary knew that what works for one person won't necessarily work for another. In effect, he was teaching me that the road to real growth is through trial and error, through working with your swing and figuring out what you can and can't depend on to come through for you. It's good to draw on the knowledge of others, but real-life skills are developed through experience—through doing, not just hearing.

I took that advice to heart and began strengthening my skills through hard work and effort. Often I'd find myself with a lie or angle that really had me baffled, and I'd hit it over and over again, trying to figure out the best way to overcome it. At one time during my career, I actually went to a lake on the course and dropped balls in the water along the edge at varying depths and lies. I'd place them one and two and three inches deep in the water, and then practice blasting them out onto the green. The drill paid off for me. Shortly afterward, during the Memorial tournament at Dublin, Ohio, I had three different water explosion shots on the front nine alone. Because I had practiced those shots, I was able to get two of them up and down and the third one on the green.

I began carrying a little black book with me on the course to keep a log of my shots. When I pulled off a difficult shot, I'd make a note in my book about how I did it, cataloging the best approaches to getting out of specific problems or obstacles.

I'd also make a note when I would come to a shot I couldn't seem to get past. There were times when I tried over and over to get out of trouble on the course but couldn't seem to make it work. I'd make a note of my difficulty, then later I would take my problem to people I trusted and ask their advice. I could always count on Gary for help. I'd take my little book to him and say, "I'm really stumped about this situation. What kind of shot would you use to pull it off?" He'd always be thrilled to give me a tip or a drill I could try, and the next time I made it to the course I'd practice the shot again until I knew I had found the solution. Then when a similar shot appeared, I had the knowledge and technique to do what I needed to do.

Through this process, I was able to sharpen my skill on the course and increase my confidence when difficult times arose. As the old sage Abe Mitchel once said, "Practice will make you wise."

In golf and in life, we need to see trying situations as building blocks for the future. Each time we come to a hazard or complication, we should use it to our advantage—as a way of increasing our skills and abilities to overcome. Each time we play a course, we are bound to find trouble. If we depend on our instincts to get us through, we will likely only end up in more rough. But if we draw on experience—what has worked in the past, for us and for others—we will have a much better chance of pulling it off.

Paul wrote, "But we also rejoice in our sufferings, because we know that suffering produces perseverance; perseverance, character;

and character, hope. And hope does not disappoint us, because God has poured out his love into our hearts by the Holy Spirit, whom he has given us" (Rom. 5:3–5).

Effective and real growth comes through embracing the bad times as well as the good. When we understand that hazards will inevitably come our way, we are more likely to prepare for them, to practice what we will do and say when they arise, to teach ourselves the best approach to overcoming the many obstacles that life and Satan will put before us. And through those experiences we develop confidence—not in ourselves, but in the one who has given us the strength and skill to move past our present situation and on to a better place.

Like Paul, we should see times of suffering as a building block to true Christian character.

20

ALWAYS CARRY A
COURSE JOURNAL

Years ago, while playing on the tour, I learned the importance of carrying a course journal. At first I kept track of my overall performance on the course—how many putts I made per hole, which clubs I used off the tee and in play, how many fairways I hit, and so on. I wanted to get a feel for my strengths and weaknesses.

But as time went by, I began to see the amazing benefits of this practice, so my journaling became more specific. I started logging every aspect of the game that I thought might help me improve. I wrote down the particulars of each shot, noting facts about the lie and distance to the pin, the potential obstacles I had to work around, which club I used, and how the shot turned out. I began cataloging these course journals and using them as barometers of my overall success.

After ten or fifteen rounds, I would compile the data I'd gathered and use it to produce my own statistics sheets. This allowed me to see at a glance my strengths and weaknesses as a player. I could see how many putts I was averaging per hole and how that part of my game was working for me. I'd know which long irons needed the most work and which ones were playing well.

Keeping a course journal proved to be invaluable to the overall success and improvement of my game. Not only did it give me a snapshot of my strengths and weaknesses, but it also provided me with an objective way to gauge my progress as time went on. I could refer back to my course journal to see how my game had improved and which areas had seen the least improvement.

> **MORE THAN SIXTY YEARS AGO, I BEGAN WRITING NOTES AND OBSERVATIONS IN WHAT I CAME TO CALL MY LITTLE RED BOOK.**
>
> HARVEY PENICK

When I became an instructor, I took those experiences and created and published a journal for students to carry with them to the course. I developed a detailed log that works for any course. I encourage my students to fill in the specifics of each hole and then log his or her performance on each shot. After ten rounds, they can take the journals and compile and average their statistics onto a master sheet. This practice gives them all the information they need to improve their game and track their progress. It works for my students as well as it worked for me.

There are two good reasons why every player should keep a course journal. The first is that we need an objective way to gain information about our game, so we will know what we need to practice on. And the second is that it helps us remember the shots we've pulled off, so we can be better prepared to repeat them in the future.

No business can survive without a business plan. Any successful entrepreneur can tell you the importance of having specific long- and short-range goals, as well as regular checks and balances to gauge how well the company is staying on track. It is the only proven method to know where you are going and how to get there.

A course journal is nothing more than a golfer's business plan. It is a way of setting goals and tracking your progress as you work to achieve them. It is an important and integral part of any good golf program.

KEEPING A SPIRITUAL JOURNAL

I have another journal I keep off the course, and I consider it far more crucial and important to the success of my life than anything I've ever done in golf.

For as long as I can remember, I've made a habit of keeping spiritual journals. Each morning during my time alone with the Lord, I try to spend some time writing out my thoughts and experiences. In fact, the books I've had the privilege of writing, including this one, have come out of the thoughts I've penned during these times of personal devotion and communion with the Lord. I journal my strengths and weaknesses as a follower of Christ. I write about specific struggles I happen to be going through and how these problems are affecting my walk of faith. I log my victories and the things I'm grateful for. I write down my prayers and the desires of my heart, expressing my innermost needs and ambitions. And I share my doubts and insecurities as a husband, father, and believer.

> **THE JOURNAL IS A PLACE TO RECORD INSIGHTS AND THOUGHTS THAT APPLY TO EACH DAY AND TO OUR LIFE IN GENERAL. IT'S ALSO A WONDERFUL RECORD OF OUR LIFE.**
>
> JIM SHEARD

There's nothing too secret or sacred for my spiritual journal. Whatever I am going through in my life, I log it in this special and personal ledger. And each day I lift up those thoughts to God. I lay everything at his feet—my cares, worries, failures, and successes—and I trust him to use those experiences to make me stronger.

There's something inherently effective and practical about keeping a daily spiritual journal. It allows us to track our strong and weak points as followers and gives us a clear barometer of our daily walk.

When we're consistent in the task, we are able to visibly gauge how we are doing, what we need to work on, and how we need to go about strengthening our relationship with God and others. We can see recurring problem areas and better know how to target those weaknesses. We can track our percentages and see which areas of our lives are not working well for us. And we can see those areas that have grown stronger and more confident over time.

But perhaps the greatest reward of keeping a daily ledger is being able to look back through time and see how God has used our transparency and faithfulness to help us grow and develop in character. We can see how he has taken our fears and walked us through them. We can track the many prayers we've lifted up—often during times of total confusion and helplessness—and see how he helped us move through those times and brought us out the other end stronger and tougher than before.

We can also see the areas in which there has been much too little growth on our part. And reviewing our journal gives us a clear indication of those things we are holding back from God—those hidden sins and transgressions we have yet to deal with effectively. We see how those things have affected other areas of our life and kept us from living up to our full potential as believers.

If you are serious about your walk with the Lord, let me strongly encourage you to begin keeping a spiritual journal today. Allow God to grow you as a Christian, to mold you in strength and character, to shine a bold light on the weaknesses and failures of your game. Let him reveal his will for your life through this simple but effective tool.

In my opinion, a spiritual journal is a critical and invaluable ingredient to any follower's walk with God. I've seen how it's worked in my life, and I know it can do the same for you.

PART 4

MENTAL AGILITY

*This should be the motto of every golfer. "If one man
conquer in battle a thousand times a thousand men,"
says the Dhammapada, with oriental extravagance,
"and if another conquer himself, he is the greatest of
conquerors"—a text which is brought home to one in
every round. "Greater," said Solomon, "is he that ruleth
himself than he that taketh a city." In golf the ruler of
himself will take many a hole.*

ARNOLD HAULTAIN

*We create success or failure on the course
primarily by our thoughts.*

GARY PLAYER

*Golf is a curious game in being easy to comprehend,
yet long in its realization.*

PERCY BOOMER

*In golf you have to concentrate. My father and
my friends call it zoning. If you mis-hit a shot,
you have to get your focus back. You have got
to start thinking ahead. Don't look back.*

TIGER WOODS

21

PLAY YOUR
OWN GAME

B ack in the '70s a young player who wanted desperately to be the
next Ben Hogan made his way onto the PGA tour. He had idol-
ized Hogan since he was a child, and he decided that the best way
to play like him would be simply to imitate him in every way possible. He practiced like Hogan, walked like Hogan, even dressed like
Hogan, wearing the characteristic white cap that Hogan was known
so well for. When this young player hit a shot, his reactions and
antics seemed to come right out of a Ben Hogan newsreel.

The problem was, this kid was not Hogan, and his game
reflected that fact. He didn't have the same skill or finesse with a
club, so he didn't last long on the tour.

The guy had great potential as a player; he just hadn't worked
to find his own game and identity. He spent so much time compar-
ing himself to Ben Hogan that he was never able to develop his own
particular style and strength on the course. As a result, he ended up
as just another flash in the pan on tour.

By its nature, golf is an intensely individual sport. To play well, it's important to recognize that fact and work to find your own specific personality and bent on the course. I'd love to have John Daly's length off the tee, but I don't have his strength or flexibility—not to mention his large, powerful frame. It would be great to have Vijah Singh's amazing accuracy with a long iron, Phil Mickelson's finesse with a 60-degree wedge, or Tiger's unbelievable skill with a putter, but I wasn't blessed with any of those things. What I do have, though, is a strong sense of my own strengths and weaknesses and an ability to play my own game in spite of what others around me are doing.

> **DO YOUR BEST, ONE SHOT AT A TIME AND THEN MOVE ON. REMEMBER THAT GOLF IS JUST A GAME.**
>
> NANCY LOPEZ

It would be easy to get caught up in jealousy over those who have more wins or greater skills than I do. To be honest, at times I have struggled with this. But I've found that the best approach is simply to be happy for the skills I do have and not focus on the ones I don't. I've learned to play my own game and let others play theirs. Taking any other attitude to the course only leads to resentment and frustration.

USING OUR SPIRITUAL GIFTS

Tony Campolo, a well-known writer and speaker, has written of the time he was asked to speak at a small country church in Indiana. He arrived early at the building to make some last-minute preparations for his sermon and noticed an elderly gentleman buzzing about the auditorium. The man carefully checked each thermostat and then opened the windows of the sanctuary slightly to let some air in. Then he went up and down each aisle to make sure all the hymnals and Bibles were neat and in order. As he walked by, Campolo said to him, "You must be the custodian."

"No," the man answered, "I'm just exercising a special gift of the Spirit."

Campolo was intrigued by his answer, so he asked the man exactly which gift of the Spirit he believed God had given him.

"The gift of helps," the man answered proudly. "Check it out in 1 Corinthians 12:28. You'll find it there. Paul talks about the gift of helps."

Campolo opened his Bible, looked up the passage, and saw that the man was right. "And in the church God has appointed first of all apostles, second prophets, third teachers, then works of miracles, also those having gifts of healing, those able to help others, those with gifts of administration, and those speaking in different kinds of tongues."

The man went on to say, "You know we get a whole parade of preachers coming through here on their way to bigger and better things. Each of them stays for a few years and then moves on. Each of them thinks that he's the best thing that this church has ever seen, and each of them thinks he's going to put this church on the map. Well, after they're gone for a few years, we have a hard time even remembering their names."

Then, pointing to himself, he continued with a wide grin, "One of these days ole Harry's goin' to die, and the people of this church won't know what hit them. They'll come to church the next Sunday and find that nobody turned up the heat. They'll find out the hard way who shoveled the snow on all those winter days. And they'll take forever to figure out where half the stuff they need to run this church is stored away."[1]

It seems that Harry had a pretty good sense of his role in the church body. And he didn't shy away from telling people about it.

We've all been given unique and special talents to be used in God's service. Scripture speaks clearly about the importance of learning our spiritual gifts and employing them within the body of Christ in order that God may be glorified. Paul wrote again about this in his

---

[1]Tony Campolo, *How to Be Pentecostal without Speaking in Tongues* (Dallas: Word, 1991), 34–35.

letter to the Ephesian church: "It was he who gave some to be apostles, some to be prophets, some to be evangelists, and some to be pastors and teachers, to prepare God's people for works of service, so that the body of Christ may be built up" (Eph. 4:11–12).

When each of us works to use our specific gifts within the body, the whole church is edified. It brings a healthy balance to Christ's kingdom on earth and allows us to reach a level of effectiveness and unity that otherwise might never be accomplished. We were created with different talents and roles for a good reason.

> IF A MAN CLEANSES HIMSELF FROM THE LATTER, HE WILL BE AN INSTRUMENT FOR NOBLE PURPOSES, MADE HOLY, USEFUL TO THE MASTER AND PREPARED TO DO ANY GOOD WORK.
>
> 2 TIMOTHY 2:21

But equally important with knowing and utilizing our gifts is that we learn to be content with whatever role God has given us. Regardless of our task within God's plan, we are invaluable to that plan as we fulfill our role in helping accomplish God's greater goal.

At times I may wish I had the speaking ability of Charles Swindoll or Billy Graham, the mind of R. C. Sproul, or the writing skills of Max Lucado, but I probably never will have. Maybe you won't either. But the gifts that you and I do have are just as crucial. Where would a church be without ushers, song leaders, nursery workers, Sunday school teachers, and custodians? For the whole to be effective, each part must function properly.

Paul addressed this issue to the church at Corinth. "Now the body is not made up of one part but of many. If the foot should say, 'Because I am not a hand, I do not belong to the body,' it would not for that reason cease to be part of the body. . . . But in fact God has arranged the parts in the body, every one of them, just as he wanted them to be. If they were all one part, where would the body be? As it is, there are many parts, but one body" (1 Cor. 12:14–15, 18–20).

The key to a successful church is for each of us to learn our specific role and to carry it out to the best of our ability—to use the gifts we do have and not worry about the ones we don't have. Any other approach only leads to jealousy and frustration.

FIND YOUR OWN FAITH

I don't believe there is another sport on earth that has generated the amount of instructional material as golf has. Everywhere you look you find golfing videos, books, tapes, and magazines—each guaranteed to help reduce your score and fix your swing. This is not surprising, given that golf is such a popular and difficult game. I'm not bothered by this phenomenon; in fact, I've created a lot of instructional material myself. I just hope people keep this material in the right perspective.

First of all, the only thing that can guarantee you a better game is hard work and practice. When asked once about the key to playing better golf, Ben Hogan said, "The secret's in the dirt. Dig it out like I did." There is no quick shortcut to lower scores.

Second, it's important to remember that no two golfers have the same game. What works for one person may completely throw another person off. We have different body types, personalities, and mental agilities, and our games should reflect that fact. Instructional material is not intended to define within us a perfect swing but to give us a foundation upon which to build our skills. The temptation for a lot of us is to try and manipulate our minds and bodies to fit into the mold of whatever instructor we are reading or listening to at the time. In effect, we are trying to play their game, instead of finding our own. The problem with this is that most golf instructors are tall, young, and lanky, with the flexibility of Gumby. Most of us are not built that way and will never be able to match their swing.

That's the main reason I rely so much on mental images in my teaching—both on the lesson tee and in my books and videos. I want students to feel their way through the swing, not to do it the way I do. This helps them find and create their own unique swing pattern and frees them to relax and focus on the results instead of on the mechanics.

My advice is not to shy away from instruction but to take the advice you get and try to integrate it into your game as it applies—to use the wisdom of others to help strengthen your own unique set of skills and abilities.

> **A HOLY LIFE ISN'T THE AUTOMATIC CONSEQUENCE OF READING THE RIGHT BOOKS, LISTENING TO THE RIGHT TAPES, OR ATTENDING THE RIGHT MEETINGS. IT'S THE RESULT OF A LIVING, LOVING UNION WITH JESUS CHRIST AND A LIFE MARKED BY GODLY DISCIPLINE.**
>
> WARREN WIERSBE

That same advice applies when reading or listening to Christian teachers and authors. The marketplace is overrunning with material for believers, each promising to help us grow deeper and stronger in our faith. This is a good and positive dynamic, because it shows that people are serious about their walk with the Lord. But it's important to use such material the way it is intended—as tools to help us grow in our personal relationship with God.

Healthy growth doesn't come through blindly following the opinions and positions of someone we respect, but through taking their counsel and integrating it into our own Christian walk as it applies. We should use their material to strengthen our faith and character, not to define them.

22

DEALING WITH ADVERSITY

Years ago I heard the story of a rookie player who had worked his way up to the lead in a tournament going into the final round. He was playing some of the best golf of his life, and it looked like he might win. Coming to the seventeenth tee box, he led the rest of the pack by several strokes.

Then on the seventeenth, he hit an errant drive that ended up in the woods, right at the base of a tree. He didn't want to take a drop and lose a stroke, so he opted to try and hit it and get it back into play. His club grounded on the tree trunk and knocked the ball sideways into another tree. He tried again and hit yet a third tree, but this time the ball bounced backward, almost knocking him in the head. Finally, he got the ball back on the fairway and was able to come away from the hole with an 8. It knocked him out of contention, back to third or fourth place.

In the locker room after the tournament, the young rookie was changing next to a bunch of old pros, and he couldn't stop complaining about his poor luck on the course. He went up and down the room, whining about the events of the seventeenth hole, telling the story over and over to anyone who would listen. "If only I had taken a drop on that first shot," he grumbled, "I might have been able to come away with a bogey. I can't believe I didn't do that. Or maybe I should have used another club to pitch it out of the tree."

DON'T LET THE BAD SHOTS GET TO YOU. DON'T LET YOURSELF BECOME ANGRY. THE TRUE SCRAMBLERS ARE THICK-SKINNED. AND THEY ALWAYS BEAT THE WHINERS.

PAUL RUNYAN

For thirty minutes the rookie bemoaned his loss to the old veterans as they sat around the bar having a few beers and trying to relax. Finally, one of the old pros got tired of the boy's ranting and said to him, "Let me tell you something, kid. We're not really interested in hearing about your bad luck. Half of the guys in here don't really care about your 8 on the seventeenth hole, and the other half wish you had made a 9."

The rookie got the message and quietly got changed. After that experience, he no doubt learned to keep his problems to himself.

Years ago I was sitting around the clubhouse with a few guys when one of them handed me his business card. His name was Frank, and he told me that whenever someone complained about their game, he would hand them one of his cards. On the back it read, "Your story has touched my heart. Never before have I heard of such appalling misfortune on the golf course. Please accept this expression of my sincere sympathy."

I almost fell out of my chair from laughing so hard. I've kept that card for over twenty years, and it still makes me smile. And it reminds me to keep my troubles to myself when I've had a bad round.

That's a good lesson for all of us. When we're struggling on the course or going through an unlucky streak, it doesn't do any good to complain. Most people really don't care about how poorly we play. On the course it's a good idea to keep your failures—and your successes—to yourself. Play your own game, and leave others alone to play theirs.

DON'T DWELL ON ADVERSITY

Keeping our problems to ourselves is a good idea in our personal life as well. We've all been around people who can't seem to keep their problems to themselves. They moan and complain constantly about the poor hand that life has dealt them— the sicknesses and ailments that plague them daily, the setbacks in their career, the persecution they suffer at the hands of others. Each new dilemma is another round of ammunition in their arsenal of unfairness.

> PRIDE IS THE DEIFICATION OF SELF, AND THIS TODAY IN SOME OF US IS NOT OF THE ORDER OF THE PHARISEE, BUT OF THE PUBLICAN. TO SAY "OH, I'M NO SAINT," IS ACCEPTABLE TO HUMAN PRIDE, BUT IT IS UNCONSCIOUS BLASPHEMY AGAINST GOD.
>
> OSWALD CHAMBERS

If you attend church regularly, you've probably run across a number of these people. They corner you in the hallway, and the minute you ask them how they are, they begin to unload a fury of grievances. "Fred still hasn't found work, and the insurance is about to run out. My back is still acting up, but how can we afford a chiropractor with no money coming in? The kids are too busy with their own lives to care, so we don't bother them anymore." Within a few minutes you are more depressed than ever.

"But don't worry about me," they continue. "I'll make it through this. I always do. I don't know how we'll get by, but we'll make it somehow."

The biggest problem I have with people who tend to have this type of persecution complex is that it shows a tremendous lack of faith in God. If we really believe God is in control, then we don't spend our days fretting over the troubles that come our way. We instead focus on what he might want to accomplish through the trials, either in our lives or in the lives of others. No one is edified by our consistent grumbling.

The truth is, at its core, complaining is really a form of pride—the worst form, in fact. It is a way of drawing attention to ourselves. Most of us think of a prideful person as one who puffs his chest and brags about himself and his accomplishments. And that certainly is true. But the most common form of pride is self-degradation. When we constantly fret over the cares and afflictions that come our way, we are really trying to keep the focus on our own personal problems instead of on God's ability to work through them. It is little more than a backhanded way of staying in the center of attention.

In fact, the pastor of our church, Joel Hunter, has often said that anxiety is actually a form of atheism. It indicates how little we trust God's authority and control in our lives.

The best approach to dealing with problems is to keep them to ourselves and let God work through them. True faith is being able to lay all of our cares and worries at the feet of Jesus and focus instead on the many blessings he has given us.

Of course, we all need to have a few people in our lives we can confide in and trust to pray for us during trying times. But beyond that, we should let our speech and attitude be positive and uplifting.

JOE KIRKWOOD'S CREDO

The late Joe Kirkwood, a famous trick-shot artist from the early 1940s and '50s, used to have a business card that he would pass out, and on the back was printed this poem:

> *Tell your story of hard luck shots,*
>   *Of each shot straight and true,*
> *But when you are done, remember, son,*
>   *Nobody cares but you.*

Before his death, Kirkwood also had that poem chiseled into his tombstone.

FIND INTERNAL SIGNIFICANCE

I was once asked to speak at a Christian men's luncheon, and while waiting to give my talk, I watched a number of men take to the podium to give their personal testimonies. Most were businessmen in the area, and they had wonderful stories about how God had blessed them financially and spiritually. One by one they got up to tell how God had opened the floodgates on their lives and careers—stories of new contracts, better jobs, bigger bonuses, more fruitful investments.

It was a great group of guys, and I loved hearing about the things God was doing for them, but somehow it all felt a bit strange. I wondered about some of the men who sat silently as the others spoke—the ones who had no stories to tell. What about the man in the audience who just lost his job, or watched his portfolio collapse? What about the guy who just found out his wife had cancer, or his business was on the verge of bankruptcy? How do these men feel when they hear stories of how God is raining his blessings on others?

> **BLESSED ARE THE POOR IN SPIRIT, FOR THEIRS IS THE KINGDOM OF HEAVEN.**
>
> JESUS (MATT. 5:3)

The truth is, God's blessing can't always be measured in material gain. Sometimes he blesses us through trials and tribulations. God doesn't measure worth and significance the way we usually do, so he will often bring tough situations into our lives in order to strengthen us and draw us closer to him. When we feel the strain of trouble in our lives, maybe God is using it to teach us trust and dependence. When it seems we are at the end of our rope, maybe God is extending his hand, waiting for us to grab hold and let him pull us through.

It's easy to fall into the trap of believing that when things are going well in our lives, it is because God is shining his grace on us, and when things are going bad, God is somehow unhappy with us. Too often we associate blessing with financial and physical success.

But God's ways are not that simple. He is not interested in how much we own, but in how much he owns within us.

On the golf course, people tend to wrap up their significance in how well they play, when a better measure would actually be how much they are growing and getting out of the game.

The same holds true in life. It's not how easily we get through each day, but how much we learn and grow spiritually in the process.

Don't Worry about Things You Can't Control

During the early '80s I was really struggling with my game. I'd had a number of pretty successful finishes through the years, but for some reason my game had started to deteriorate, and I found myself in something of a slump. The season had not gone well for me, and as fall approached I realized I was in danger of losing my card. There were only two tournaments left for the year, and I had to make a good amount of money during those rounds in order to gain a spot for the next season. Otherwise I'd have to go back to qualifying school and try to get back on the tour. It was not a great feeling.

> YOU TEND TO GET IMPATIENT WITH LESS-THAN-PERFECT SHOTS, BUT YOU HAVE TO REMEMBER THAT LESS-THAN-PERFECT SHOTS WIN OPENS.
>
> CURTIS STRANGE

My chances came down to the last day of the season, at Pensacola. I knew that I needed to shoot at least a 69 for the day to put me far enough up on the money list to keep my card. By the eighth hole I was already 2 over par. It didn't look promising.

Walking toward the ninth tee box, I found myself completely exasperated. I began thinking to myself, *What am I going to do now?* I was convinced there was no way I could recover before the end of the round, so I began to go over my options. *I don't want to face another year of qualifying school*, I thought. *Maybe I should just get a job at a club somewhere. Or maybe I need to go into another line of work. I'm obviously not cut out for the PGA tour.* I was at the end of my rope and emotionally beaten to the ground.

Then while standing on the ninth tee box, a strange thing happened. For some reason a clear and distinct thought popped into my mind: *What's the difference between a birdie and a bogey a hundred years from now?* The thought seemed to come out of nowhere, but it really got my attention.

I told my caddy, Buzz, about it, and he said, "That's a good way to look at it. Just do your best. A hundred years from now no one will care what you shot."

I knew I had ten holes to go, and I committed that moment to stop worrying about what would happen and just play my best. I stood on the tenth tee box before my shot and said aloud, "What's the difference between a birdie and a bogey a hundred years from now?" Then I took my shot—a beautiful drive right down the middle. My next shot was a 9-iron, and as I stood over the ball, I said the phrase again, this time a little

> REMEMBER—YOU HAVE TO BE COMFORTABLE. GOLF IS NOT A LIFE OR DEATH SITUATION. IT'S JUST A GAME AND SHOULD BE TREATED AS SUCH.
>
> CHI CHI RODRIGUEZ

under my breath. "What's the difference between a birdie and a bogey a hundred years from now?" Then I took my swing and the ball sailed right into the hole for an eagle!

I was playing with two great guys that day, Larry Rinker and Gary Hallberg, and they were thrilled for me. We high-fived each other on the green and then made our way to the tenth hole. For the rest of the day, I made a habit of repeating that statement before each shot. My game turned completely around. Larry and Gary had already earned their cards for the following year, and they spent much of the round rooting for me. Their encouragement, along with my fresh outlook and perspective, allowed me to relax and play the way I knew I was capable of playing. I ended up shooting a 67 for the day, and that was all I needed to regain my spot on the tour.

In golf, as in life, it's easy to get caught up wallowing in self-pity when things don't go our way. We spend a lot of time fretting over things that are not that important in the grand scheme of life—usually things that we have little control over anyway. And every now and then we need to be reminded that regardless of what happens, God is in control. He is right beside us, whispering in our ear, "You're right where you're supposed to be. Just trust me and it will work out."

Besides, what's the difference between a birdie and a bogey a hundred years from now anyway?

23

WORK WITH WHAT YOU HAVE

I cut my teeth in golf on a small nine-hole course in my hometown of Oaklandon, Indiana. The course had only a couple of sand traps, and they were filled with hard, midwestern dirt. To get out of the traps, you had to either chip the ball softly or roll it out with a putter. Neither was a great alternative, so we avoided those two traps like the plague.

As a result, when I went on to play golf in college I had almost no experience playing out of sand traps. It was obvious to me and everyone else that this created a serious deficiency in my game, so I began practicing sand shots at every opportunity, but I never quite learned to be comfortable hitting out of the sand. I knew that if I ever had hopes of playing on tour, I would need to overcome this problem.

After a brief stint in the military, I went to southern Florida to take on the grueling, six-round, PGA qualifying school. As I looked out over the first course, I couldn't believe all the sand. In places it seemed as if I were looking out over a desert. The course was beautifully landscaped and lined with trees down every fairway, and I couldn't wait to play it. But every hole abounded with huge, gaping bunkers. I couldn't remember the last time I had felt so intimidated by a course.

In spite of my best efforts to steer clear of the sand, early in the round I found myself in a large, deep bunker around the green. As I stood surveying the shot, I considered my options. At first I was just trying to figure out the best approach to blasting it out of the sand and getting it to stick on the green. The walls were high and looming, and I knew I'd need to make solid contact. But then I noticed a low place in the lip ahead of me. The sand was pretty firm, and I thought if I could just get good contact and aim well, I could putt it right over that lip and onto the green. I decided to give it a try. My gamble paid off. I hit a perfect putt that rolled the ball up over the lip, through the rough, and onto the green, ending up about four feet from the pin.

> **HIT THE SHOT YOU KNOW YOU CAN HIT, NOT THE ONE YOU THINK YOU SHOULD.**
>
> BOB ROTELLA

My playing partner couldn't believe his eyes. In the clubhouse later that day, he couldn't stop telling people about my up and down from the sand with a putter.

I always knew that someday I would need to learn how to play a proper sand shot. In fact, I wanted to be really good at it, and I was willing to put in the hours of practice it would take to do so. But until that time, I had to make do with the skills I had.

Growing up playing on a poorly designed course didn't allow me to learn all I needed to know about tour-level golf, but what I lacked in ability I made up for in ingenuity. I learned to be creative on the course and to work through trying situations the best I could. Instead of worrying about the skills I didn't have, I depended on the ones I did have. In the end it proved to only add to my strength as a player.

After gaining my card three years later, one of the first tournaments I played was at Pebble Beach. While there, I ran across my old friend and former employer, Gary Player. Gary was the best sand player I'd ever seen, and I longed to have his skills out of the traps. I looked in his bag to see what kind of sand wedge he was using and noticed he had an old 1953 Wilson Staff club, so I went out and found one just like it. In fact, I found two and acquired them both. (It wasn't long afterward that I got a tap on my shoulder from Tom Watson, asking if he could have one of them. He'd been looking in Gary's bag as well and had been trying to locate the same wedge. I often wonder if that was the wedge he used to chip in at Pebble Beach to win the U.S. Open!)

> NO BUNKER SHOT HAS EVER SCARED ME, AND NONE EVER WILL. THE KEY TO THIS BRAVADO IS PRACTICE.
>
> GARY PLAYER

Over the months and years to come, I worked tirelessly to learn how to hit all kinds of shots out of the sand. I was committed to being the best sand player I could possibly be. In time my skills began to improve, and I was making a lot of progress. Often Gary and I would hook up before a tournament and play practice rounds. We'd spend hours dropping and burying balls in the traps and hitting them out, each time trying to enhance our skills a bit more.

Today I am not only a good sand player, but it is one of the strengths of my game. Throughout my career I've made many a good save because of my skills and ingenuity in and around the bunkers. What started out as a serious deficiency in my game eventually became one of my greatest assets as a player.

We all have strengths and weaknesses. Some golfers have an amazing long game and can putt it in from anywhere on the green, but their short irons always give them problems. In spite of this weakness, they are able to keep up with other players because they've learned to capitalize on the skills they do have and to work around the ones they don't.

I've always been good around the greens, and I've saved many a hole by chipping it close from very difficult lies and positions. Through hard work and practice, I was able to turn my greatest weakness into one of my strengths. In fact, later in my career I often found myself looking forward to difficult lies in the sand, because it gave me an opportunity to utilize the skills I had developed.

I learned that a great short game improves all of your shots. When you know you can get up and down from around the green, you have the confidence to attempt shots with your woods and long irons that you might not otherwise try.

In golf there is no one way to play. The goal is to get the ball into the cup in as few strokes as possible, and whatever works toward that end is a valid strategy—even if it means taking a Texas wedge out of the sand.

A CREATIVE SHOT

There's a great story told about Ben Hogan playing in a tournament at Pebble Beach. The infamous seventh hole on that course is a short par-3 playing toward the ocean. It's a tiny green about a hundred yards downhill, with a bunker along the front edge. The wind at Pebble Beach often blew so hard it was hard to stand up on the tee box. Players had been known to take a 2-iron off the tee and hit into the wind, just to get it to the green.

As Hogan stood on that tee box assessing the shot, the wind was blowing so hard no one could imagine how he was going to pull off his shot. He surprised the gallery by taking out his putter and aiming for the trap in front of the green. He putted the ball all the way down the fairway and into the bunker for a safe second shot toward the pin.

It was vintage Hogan creativity.

There are times in my walk with Christ when I think I understand what Hogan must have felt like standing on that tee box with a gale force wind in his face. Often I'll be going through my day as planned, moving from one task to the next, when suddenly I find myself faced with a situation that seems insurmountable. I have no idea what to do next and am left wondering how I'm going to get past this obstacle that the enemy has put in my way.

When these situations arise, the key is to keep a cool head and not panic. Sometimes you have to think outside of the box. When faced with adversity, Hogan knew that he could call on the many skills he had honed through the years, even if that meant pulling a shot out of his bag that he'd never tried before. As a believer, I need to be willing to look at my faith in that same manner.

In 2 Timothy 3:16, Paul wrote, "All Scripture is God-breathed and is useful for teaching, rebuking, correcting and training in righteousness, *so that the man of God may be thoroughly equipped* for every good work" (italics mine).

Our time with God—in prayer and in the Word—should equip us for any task or obstacle the enemy may put in front of us. It's our job to stay calm and look to God, instead of our own strength, when troubling times come our way.

Sometimes our greatest triumph comes in the midst of our most overwhelming hardship.

24

PLAY WITHIN YOURSELF

One of the most difficult things a player has to do on the golf course is to stay involved in his own game and not get caught up in watching someone else play. The tendency a lot of players have is to compare their game with that of their playing partners. Most golfers are competitive by nature, so this is a natural trap to fall into, but it can easily throw your round off—especially if your partner is better than you and maybe getting a lot of good breaks on the course.

It's hard to stay involved in your own game plan when the guy next to you is outdriving you by fifty yards and getting more distance out of every iron in his bag. The temptation to try to keep up with them is more than most golfers can handle, so they overwind the club and swing out of their shoes in an effort to match them. More often than not, it only leads to disaster.

This temptation is highly understandable, since golfers tend to put so much emphasis on long drives off the tee. By nature, golfers are fascinated by people who can crush the ball three hundred yards down the fairway, like Tiger Woods and John Daly. But those guys would be the first to tell you that games are won and lost by what happens around the greens, not by long tee shots. As Harvey Penick once said, "The woods are full of long drivers."

> **MY STRATEGY? PLAYING SAFE AND WITHIN MYSELF.**
>
> BILLY CASPER

The key is to fight the urge to keep up with others and simply play your own game—to know your personal skills and abilities and play within those perimeters. That's why it's so important to come to the course with a game plan laid out in your mind. It gives you a concrete plan of action to follow and keeps guesswork out of the equation. But it won't work for you unless you can ignore what's going on around you and stick to it.

Lower scores happen when players learn to put distractions and obstacles completely out of their mind and focus on the task or shot at hand. And that means knowing what you can and can't do with a particular club at a given point and time. You weigh your skills and abilities against the options before you and then make a decision based on the play that will give you the best chance of being in a good position to score. In golf your most important rival is the course and the scorecard. Your goal is not to beat other players but to beat the course better than other players are able to on a given day.

Play within yourself and your abilities, and you'll have the best shot at doing just that.

EVEN PROS GET DISTRACTED

High-handicappers aren't the only ones who fall into the trap of trying to keep up with their playing partners. I've seen it happen to players at all levels of the game.

I remember watching a tournament several years ago during Tiger Wood's first season on the PGA tour. During the third round he was paired with John Daly. The crowd that gathered to follow them around the course was almost unbelievable. It seemed everyone wanted to get a view of the two longest drivers on tour playing against each other.

One of the holes on the front nine was a long par-5 that dog-legged sharply to the left. The fairway was wide for the first 250 yards and then narrowed into a small gap between masses of trees towering on either side. The fairway turned left just beyond the trees. Players had two options—they could either lay up with a long iron and pitch over the trees on their second shot, giving them a wedge into the green, or they could try to land a perfect tee shot right into the pocket of the narrow fairway between the trees, giving them a chance to carry the green in two. The latter option was extremely risky. If you missed the pocket, you'd be hitting out of the woods.

> SMART GOLF IS WINNING GOLF. CUT DOWN ON THE ELEMENT OF CHANCE.
>
> WALTER HAGEN

Daly was the first up, and few were surprised to see him with a driver in his hands. Daly is known well for his go-for-broke attitude—which is both his strength and his weakness. To the delight of the crowd, he hit an unbelievable drive right down the middle, which fed perfectly into the center of the pocket. The gallery went nuts with excitement.

As the camera panned over to Tiger, he was standing with a long iron in his hands. He was several strokes in the lead and was planning to lay up. After seeing what Daly had done, the crowd began taunting Tiger to match his shot. Several people in the back of the crowd started chanting, "Go for it! Go for it! Go for it!" Daly grinned and walked over to Tiger's bag. He took out Tiger's driver and handed it to him as a mock challenge.

Everyone wondered what Tiger would to do. At first it seemed as though he would stick to his game plan and lay up, but the pressure from the crowd got to him, and he grabbed his driver and walked to the tee. After a little polite exchange between the two players, he teed one up and let it rip. It didn't work out as he had hoped. He hit a great shot, but it was slightly to the right, sending the ball deep into the trees. Thankfully he was able to recover and come away with a par, but it was a tough up and down. He knew that in spite of the pressure from the crowd, he should have stuck to his original game plan. Daly's second shot came up short, and he made a par as well, showing that even the best drives don't always pay out like they promise.

KNOW WHAT'S IMPORTANT

When Scott Simpson won the 1987 U.S. Open at the Olympic Club, he was a thirty-one-year-old journeyman who had never won a major championship. Though he was respected as a player, no one expected him to be at the top of the leader board on Sunday, trading shots with Tom Watson down the homestretch. The pressure of being in the lead is more than most young players can handle, which is why so many new pros get into contention and then fall apart at the turn on the final day of a tournament. But Scott handled it beautifully.

Coming into the sixteenth hole, Simpson was one stroke ahead of Watson, who was making his way to the tee box on the fifteenth. Simpson pushed his drive into the woods and found himself in trouble. Most people expected him to pitch out into the fairway and get the ball back into play, but he surprised everyone by going for the green. The ball barely carried two bunkers and bounced softly on the apron to roll within fifteen feet of the cup—a brilliant shot, especially under the immense pressure. On the ABC broadcast, Jack Nicklaus could be heard laughing in amazement, saying, "I never thought of playing it that way." Nicklaus went on to talk about what an impact this win would have on Simpson's career and commented to the other announcers that this must be the greatest thing Simpson had ever done.

Simpson birdied the shot to go 3 under. Watson birdied the fifteenth to stay one stroke behind him. Both men parred the rest of the holes coming in, and Simpson won the tournament by one stroke.

Of all the comments made about the game that day, the one that came up most often was that Simpson seemed amazingly calm and collected throughout the round—which is no small task in any tournament, but especially difficult when you've got the great Tom Watson on your tail.

I'VE HAD THE PRIVILEGE OF SPEAKING AT THE **PGA TOUR BIBLE** STUDIES NUMEROUS TIMES, AND IT HAS BEEN A THRILL TO SEE SO MANY PLAYERS STAND UP AND SHARE THE EXCITEMENT OF THEIR RELATIONSHIP WITH JESUS CHRIST.

BILLY GRAHAM

One of the first questions Simpson was asked in the press tent was, "Scott, this has to be the most important thing you have ever done." Without hesitation, Simpson replied, "No, accepting Jesus Christ as my Savior and Lord was the most important thing I've ever done." Throughout the interview he continued to give credit for his win to his ability to keep his game in perspective and trust God for any success or failure he might have.

It was later discovered that before the round, Simpson had written a Scripture verse on the top of the scorecard he carried with him. Between each hole he read and reflected on a passage from Colossians 3:23–24: "Whatever you do, work at it with all your heart, as working for the Lord, not for men, since you know that you will receive an inheritance from the Lord as a reward. It is the Lord Christ you are serving."

This was Scott's way of reminding himself that all he could really do was play to the best of his ability and trust that the final outcome would be as God intended. He knew that winning was not that important in the grand scheme of things and that staying focused on his position before Christ was all that really mattered. That knowledge freed him to relax and simply play his game one shot at a time.

If someone were to ask you, "What's the greatest thing you've ever done?" would you be able to share with them about your relationship with God? Ultimately, what we do in our lives pales in comparison with how we stand before our Lord and Savior. It's the one decision in all of our lives that truly makes a difference.

25

REPLAY GOOD SHOTS IN YOUR MIND

When I caddied for Gary Player on the tour, the thing that stuck with me the most was his incredibly positive attitude. Every shot he came to, no matter how bad the lie or how many obstacles were in the way, he knew he could pull it off. In fact, he seemed to enjoy the difficult shots even more than the clean ones. He'd stand over the ball and gaze at the target with anticipation. You could see in his eyes he knew exactly what he needed to do and had no doubt he could do it.

Gary never took a negative thought to the course, and he expected those around him to have that same attitude. He was not an easy man to caddy for. He had very specific expectations for those who carried his bag—you had to stand a certain way, place the bag down in a specific manner on each hole, and remain a perfect distance behind him during each shot. He saw his caddy's actions as an extension of his pre-shot routine, and it had to be just right. But the most important thing he expected of his caddy was a positive attitude. He refused to hear any negative words or thoughts in his presence.

I learned early that when Gary was discussing club selection, he wasn't really looking for advice but for positive confirmation of the club he had chosen. He might say to me on a particular shot, "Looks like about a 6-iron, what do you think?" I might have questioned his choice in my mind, but I would never have dreamt of saying, "I think it's a 5." My job was to say, "Looks like a perfect 6 to me too!" Putting even a hint of doubt into the air was considered a huge breach of protocol and might have even gotten me thrown off his bag.

Gary also had a tremendous memory for shots he had hit in the past. Whenever he made a great save, he would log it deep in his memory bank for future reference, and when he came to a difficult lie or shot, he would let his mind take him back to a similar one he had made some time earlier—even years beforehand. Then he would reflect on that instance, remembering the angle and projection of the ball and the swing he used to carry it out. He visualized himself hitting that same shot, and then he'd take a club and repeat it. More often than not, he pulled it off beautifully, giving him even another great shot to remember.

> YOU NEED A FANTASTIC MEMORY TO REMEMBER THE GREAT SHOTS AND A VERY SHORT MEMORY TO FORGET THE BAD ONES.
>
> MAC O'GRADY

This practice worked wonderfully to help build his confidence and create positive thoughts in the midst of trouble. When I went on tour I started integrating this habit into my own game.

Anything that can help you create a sense of confidence on the course is worth trying. The next time you find yourself struggling with doubt over a shot, try replaying your greatest saves in your mind, and then visualize yourself repeating those same strokes. Remembering that you've pulled off difficult shots before is a great way to help you do it again.

A LASTING FRIENDSHIP

I'll never forget the day I met Dr. Everett Johnson. It was in the early '70s and I had attended a Fellowship of Christian Athletes (FCA) breakfast during the Citrus Open in Orlando. Larry Nelson was the guest speaker that day. He was new to the PGA circuit at the time and had yet to win a tournament. Larry had recently given his life to Christ, and he did a wonderful job sharing his testimony and challenging those who had not accepted Jesus as their Savior to do so.

I was called on to help with the follow-up work, and a few days after the breakfast I received a commitment card filled out by Ev Johnson. He indicated on the card that he and his wife, Elsa, had attended the breakfast that morning and had prayed along with Larry to receive Christ as their personal Lord and Savior. I had the privilege of calling on Ev and Elsa to follow up on their commitment and to ask if they had any questions.

Ev was in his mid-sixties at the time and had recently retired from his dental practice in Madison, Wisconsin. He and Elsa had a winter condo in Winter Park, Florida, where Ev was a member at Bay Hill Country Club.

Ev and I became great friends over the months and years to come. Though there was a big difference in our ages, we got together regularly for lunch and other outings, and we would while away the hours telling golf and fishing stories. Often we would completely lose track of time as we talked and laughed together. Every chance I got, I would take Ev to one of our ministry luncheons or golf tournaments. Once a month we hooked up to play together in the golf fellowship scrambles in Orlando.

As his age increased, Ev's health began to deteriorate. He developed Alzheimer's, so he wasn't able to play a round of golf like he used to. Still I took him with me to the tournaments each month. He would ride around the course with me in the cart and became my designated putter.

Eventually, as his disease worsened, he and Elsa thought it best to move back to Wisconsin to be near family. Though I hated to see him go, I knew I'd be able to see him often during my travels. At every opportunity I made my way over to Wisconsin to see Ev and Elsa.

On one occasion I flew into Madison and picked Ev up, and we drove to an FCA Junior Golf camp just sixty miles north of his home. I had been asked to give a clinic at the camp and to share my testimony and my experiences on tour with the kids. After my talk several of the campers shared their thoughts and testimonies, and it really touched Ev's heart.

Late that evening we all made our way to the bunkhouse to turn in for the night. I'll never forget seeing Ev slip on his pajamas and climb into the lower bunk beneath me. He looked just like a little kid, so sweet and innocent. Ev had an amazing heart for kids, and they all loved having him around.

> **APPROACH LIFE LIKE A VOYAGE ON A SCHOONER. ENJOY THE VIEW. EXPLORE THE VESSEL. MAKE FRIENDS WITH THE CAPTAIN. FISH A LITTLE. AND THEN GET OFF WHEN YOU GET HOME.**
>
> MAX LUCADO

While at the camp, Ev and I walked down to the lake and spent several hours talking about life, faith, and friendships. We sat on the shore and had a beautiful time of prayer and reflection. Ev shared with me that he really struggled to feel he was good enough to be accepted by God. He felt he had not done enough for the Lord in his life. Like a lot of men who come to Christ late in life, Ev had a hard time understanding that salvation is not dependent on anything we do, but only on our acceptance of God's grace and forgiveness. I spent time reassuring Ev that God accepted him exactly as he was, then we prayed again as Ev recommitted his life and heart to Jesus. Then I thanked God for the many years we had spent getting to know each other. A year later the Lord took Ev home.

God brings people like Ev into our lives for a reason. He created each of us with a deep need for binding and long-lasting relationships. Without these relationships, life would be a long and lonely road to travel, and few of us would find much joy in the journey.

It's easy to get caught up in the grind of everyday life, working and saving and acquiring possession after possession, seldom taking time to reflect on the good friends that God has placed in our lives. Too many of us spend more time mowing our yards and decorating our houses than we do laughing and enjoying the company of others. But we should never forget that when all else is said and done, it is the relationships in our lives—with God, our family, our friends, and everyone else we meet—that make us who we are and define our legacy.

Take time today to ask God to bring people into your life that will make a lasting impact on your faith and future. And then thank him for the people he has already led you to—those who bring joy and love into your life. Reflect on the times of fun and fellowship you've shared with them and the many ways they've blessed your life.

When you and I are gone, no one will remember what kind of car we drove, what tournaments we won, how low we were able to shoot, or how large a portfolio we built. But they will remember our times together—what kind of parent, spouse, friend, and believer we were during our days on earth.

In the end, that's all that really matters.

26

PUT BAD SHOTS BEHIND YOU

During my second year on the PGA tour, I found myself tied for the lead with Gary McCord during the third round of the prestigious Doral tournament in Miami, Florida. It was my first time leading a tournament. When I got the pairing sheet for Saturday's round, I saw that I was paired with Jack Nicklaus and Lee Trevino—two of the greatest players of the day—in the last grouping. I knew the crowd would be huge and the television cameras would be on us for the final holes. My mom and dad were there to watch me, and they had called all of my friends and relatives to tell them to tune in. It was an enormous amount of pressure for a young player.

Early Saturday morning, as I prepared myself for the round, I lifted my game up to the Lord and asked him to calm my nerves and help me get through it. I understood that I was still young and early in my career and that I should look at this opportunity as a chance to grow my skills for the future. Looking back, I should have had more confidence in my game, but at the time, I honestly didn't know if I could win. I just saw the tournament mostly as a chance to get some good experience playing under pressure. My prayer that morning was that God would use the round to teach me something valuable I could use in the future.

I spent most of the day throwing shots away. I couldn't seem to get my game together. With each hole I seemed to fall further behind the pack, while my playing partners continued to move ahead and fight for the lead. No matter how hard I tried, I couldn't seem to pull it together, and about halfway through the round I began getting angry. Here I was in the leading group of a tournament, in front of the biggest crowd of my career, with more television cameras around than I had ever seen, and all I could do was stink up the course. It was more than frustrating; it was downright embarrassing.

> I DON'T DWELL ON BAD SHOTS, BAD ROUNDS, OR BAD TOURNA- MENTS. I DON'T PLAY IN THE PAST. I PLAY IN THE PRESENT.
>
> RAYMOND FLOYD

On the sixteenth hole I hit a good approach shot that gave me an opportunity for a birdie. Walking up to the green, I was determined to make it count. In my mind I was cursing myself for the way I had been playing, and I decided that I was at least going to make a good showing on the last few holes—to prove that I really did belong there.

I had a putt on the same line of Nicklaus's, only a bit closer, with a slight break toward the left. I watched as Nicklaus missed his putt just to the right, and it gave me a great line. *This is one putt I should be able to make,* I thought to myself. I lined it up, carefully stroked it down the line, and it missed—slightly to the right, the same as Nicklaus's ball had done.

I was furious with myself, and everyone could see it. I stomped over to the next tee and stood with my arms folded across my chest. *How could I be so stupid?* I thought. *What am I doing to myself?* As I stepped up to the tee I still didn't have my anger under control. I pulled the club back and really laid into it, trying to crush it down the fairway, but instead I managed to push it right, deep into the rough.

I give up, I thought to myself. At this point, all I wanted to do was finish the round and go back to my room. But as I was walking down the fairway toward my ball, I suddenly felt an arm around my neck. I glanced over to see Lee Trevino staring me right in the face. He looked me in the eyes and said, "Hey son, forget about that. It's history, and you can't change it." I forced a smile and he patted me on the back and gave me a few more words of encouragement before heading toward his ball, which was nestled safely in the fairway.

At that moment I suddenly remembered my prayer early that morning. I had prayed that God would use this day to teach me a lesson and now realized he was doing just that. I just hadn't expected it to be such a hard-won lesson. Walking toward my ball, a Scripture verse came into my mind—one very similar to the words Trevino had just given me: "But one thing I do: Forgetting what is behind and straining toward what is ahead, I press on toward the goal to win the prize for which God has called me heavenward in Christ Jesus" (Phil. 3:13–14).

I finally understood what God was trying to teach me. I had been so busy worrying about impressing the crowds, the cameras, and my fellow players with my golfing ability, that I had completely forgotten why God allowed me to make it onto the tour in the first place. It wasn't so that I could fill my shelves with trophies and make a name for myself, or even that I could become the greatest golfer of my time. He put me there to have an influence on the tour for Christ. I was there to set a good example, to reach out to fans and other players, and to allow Christ's love to shine through me.

The goal that God wanted me to *press on toward* was not a string of birdies or a tournament win, but a faithful showing of his love and glory in spite of my apparent poor luck on the course.

I finished the round that day thoroughly convicted by the lesson God had taught me. I thanked Trevino for his kindness and made my way to the scoring tent with a renewed understanding of my purpose in golf. I committed that day to keep my game and life in perspective.

I told God that in the future no matter how badly I played or how poor my luck, whether on or off the course, I would always work to put it behind me and press forward. God is the one who gave me the skills and talents to make it on tour, and he is the one who controls the future of my career. My job is to simply take it one round at a time and to be a light and an example to those who may be watching.

I made a commitment that day that I would no longer take poor shots with me to the next hole, no matter how poorly I played or how bad my luck. From that time on, whenever I would have a bad experience on a specific hole, I would make a point of standing on the edge of the green and putting it out of my mind before stepping up to the next tee box. No matter what happened, I would leave it right there on the fringe and start fresh.

That simple practice made a greater difference in my mental game than anything I had ever done. During that season, I made only about 30 percent of the two-day cuts, but the following season I made over 80 percent of them.

Whether in golf or life, the principle of putting your bad shots behind you is a solid and important one. In every circumstance, we need to put our bad shots behind us and look instead to the future.

DON'T LET YOUR PAST DEFINE YOUR FUTURE

Shortly after I left the tour I found myself struggling to find an identity away from the professional golf circuit. I had a hard time adjusting to my new life and career. Much of my self-worth had been tied to the successes I'd had in golf, and now I no longer had that in my life. As a result, a lot of deeply rooted issues of insecurity were beginning to come to the surface, and I finally felt that I needed to deal with them.

I sought the help of a competent Christian counselor in our area. Though it was difficult to swallow my pride and seek the advice of a professional, I had nowhere else to turn.

As I sat one day staring out my counselor's window at leaves hanging from the gutter, he turned to me and asked, "Wally, if your father were here right now, what would you say to him? And what would you want to hear him say to you?"

> **MANY TIMES WHEN FEAR STARTS TO GET ME, MY BEST CHANCE OF OVER-COMING IT LIES IN FACING IT SQUARELY AND EXAMINING IT RATIONALLY.**
>
> JACK NICKLAUS

Almost instantly I began to fall apart. My father had died just a few years earlier, and I had never come to terms with our strained relationship. A flood of tears started rolling down my cheeks and onto the front of my shirt. I couldn't seem to gain control over my emotions. It was a completely unexpected experience on my part. Though I tried to answer my counselor's questions, my tears wouldn't stop coming. I cried through the rest of the session and into the evening hours as well.

The very next day, I was in the car traveling to Cocoa Beach for a golfing seminar. While winding down the small two-lane highway, I began fiddling with the radio knob to find some music to listen to. I happened upon the voice of Dr. James Dobson conducting one of his Focus on the Family radio programs—a program I love listening to but seldom get the chance to catch.

Within a few minutes I realized he was interviewing the child of an alcoholic father, and it immediately got my attention, so I turned the volume up a bit. Out of the blue, Dr. Dobson asked the man, "If your father were here right now, what would you want to say to him? And what would you want him to say to you?"

The same question the counselor had asked of me the day before.

Once again, my emotions began to well out of control. I didn't even hear the answer Dr. Dobson's guest gave, because I was so caught up in my own reaction. *Why was I so deeply affected by this question?* I struggled to come to grips with my emotions. I had to pull over to the side of the road to keep from causing an accident. There I sat and cried until the tears would no longer come.

You see, my father was an alcoholic and, for most of his life, an unbeliever. During my childhood I never seemed to be able to please him. He was a hard and cold man who constantly drove my family and me away from him. Most of my days as a boy were spent trying to impress my father, trying to earn his love and affection. I worked tirelessly to gain even a hint of approval, but no matter how well I did in school or sports, it never seemed to be enough.

> WHEN YOU'RE FROM AN ALCOHOLIC FAMILY, FEELINGS ARE THE FIRST THINGS TO GO. YOU LEARN TO STUFF THEM AWAY, OUT OF REACH. AND VIRTUALLY OUT OF SIGHT. BUT THEY'RE ALWAYS THERE, LURKING. LIKE YOUR SHADOW, THEY REMIND YOU THAT YOU'RE NEVER ALONE.
>
> LOUIE ANDERSON

I remember many nights of lying awake in bed, listening to my father argue with my mother. Other times, in his anger he'd begin attacking me verbally, calling me a bum, a lazy, worthless kid. Often he would scream at me and send me to my room. He accused me of not taking my golf seriously, of not practicing enough. Then when I started spending more time on the course, he'd be angry with me for not pulling my load at home or for not getting a job. No matter what I did or how hard I tried, he was never pleased.

As I sat in my car on the side of the road, crying uncontrollably, I finally understood. For the first time I had the answer to the counselor's question. The words I so longed to hear from my father were, "Wally, you tried."

It was such a simple thing, and so little to ask for, but it's all I ever wanted. I was so starved for his affection and so damaged by his coldness toward me that I didn't even expect words of love and affirmation, just a simple acknowledgement that I did my best. That I tried.

How I longed for just a few words of confirmation from my father. I yearned to hear him say just once, "Good try, Wally." But those words never came.

Looking back, I can see why I was so driven as a golfer. I was constantly pushing myself to be better, to shoot lower, to drive longer, to gain more respect from others. I had a deep need to prove my worth—both to myself and to my father. Yet in spite of my accomplishments, I was lost and miserable inside.

I understand now why a simple question would have expelled such powerful emotions from within me. I longed for something I could never gain—my father's approval. That hunger had stayed with me long into adulthood. Even today, though I have long since worked through my anger and forgiven my father for the emotional abuse he inflicted on my brothers and me, I still struggle with feelings of inadequacy.

But through the years I've learned that only God can meet my deepest longings for love and significance. Only he can heal the wounds and fill the emptiness in my heart. And through his grace and gentle words of affirmation, he has not only helped me to overcome my past but to redesign my future as well.

He can do the same for you. Whatever scars you are carrying, whatever pain you bear from the people and words of your past, let God reach in and heal them. Allow him to move you through those experiences on to greater and higher things.

Your past may affect you, but it doesn't have to define you. Let God be the source of your self-worth and inner strength. He's the Father that loves us in spite of our flaws and failures.

PART 5

THE SPIRIT OF THE GAME

*The only way of really finding out a man's true
character is to play golf with him. In no other
walk of life does the cloven hoof so quickly dis-
play itself. . . . The man who can go into a
patch of rough alone, with the knowledge that
only God is watching him, and play his ball
where it lies, is the man who will serve you
faithfully and well.*
P. G. WODEHOUSE

*I enjoyed the game because it is so similar to
the game of life, with its many obstacles,
struggles, victories, conflicts, and blessings.
If you're not modest about your abilities when
you start playing the game, it won't take long
for you to assume a role of humility—
that's the nature of the game.*
BILLY GRAHAM

Golf is a game of integrity.
RAYMOND FLOYD

27

TRUST YOUR CADDY

Golfers have always had an affection for the old courses, especially the ones in Scotland. Old Scottish courses were built with a hint of intrigue and a lot of creativity, with blind tee shots and hidden greens nestled throughout. If you don't stay on your toes, you can easily find yourself buried in a patch of thicket hiding behind a bunker or on the other side of a mound. And when you do find trouble, it's seldom easy to recover. The Scottish designers loved to trip you up—almost as much as they loved golf.

A few of the old American courses have that same element of danger. The Pine Valley course, located just across the river from Philadelphia, is one such example. It's been named as one of the top courses in the country by a number of different surveys. Many of the holes have totally blind shots over trees and ridges, and the course abounds with dips, mounds, and other obstacles.

The first time I played Pine Valley it was raining so hard I was sure the day's rounds would be canceled. During breakfast we were all waiting for the announcement of delay due to heavy rains, but it never came. Then someone came in to say that we were on the first tee.

My caddy that morning was a man named Bob. He was a local player and wore a huge, floppy hat and full rain gear down to his toes. His oversized galoshes flopped and squished as he walked with me toward the first hole.

As we started our round, the rains began to pick up. Visibility was low, and as we walked up to one of the early tee boxes—second or third, I believe—I looked out over the large, wet course and suddenly realized that I had no idea where to aim. All I could see was a wide fairway feeding into a high ridge in the distance. The green was nowhere in sight. I asked my caddy if he knew the course well enough to show me where to aim. He smiled and told me, "I'll go stand in the fairway on top of the hill, and you hit it right over my head."

IN TOURNAMENT PLAY, [MY CADDY] ALWAYS HAD A KNACK FOR KNOWING THE RIGHT THING TO SAY, EVEN WHEN THAT MEANT SAYING NOTHING AT ALL. AND HE UNDERSTOOD THE NUANCES OF COMPETITION AS WELL AS ANYONE I'D EVER MET.

NICK PRICE

He made his way down the course and stood on the mound in the distance, waving me on when he got into position. I could barely see him in the thick morning mist. I dried the grip off with a towel, wiped the rain from my forehead, took dead aim directly over Bob's head, and then made my swing. Bob watched the ball as it sailed over his head and settled into the middle of the fairway beyond him. I was in perfect position for my approach shot.

Sitting safely on the green in 2, Bob stood behind me as I lined my putt up. He told me exactly how the putt would break and how far, giving me a perfect line to the hole before stepping aside. I trusted his advice and took the stroke exactly as he had suggested. The ball fed perfectly into the cup for a birdie.

A few holes later we came to another blind shot over a hill, so Bob again made his way down the fairway to stand on top of the mound, giving me a target to aim at. And once more I found myself in perfect position for my approach shot.

Throughout the round, Bob continued to guide me through the course. I soon discovered he had been playing Pine Valley for most of his life and knew the course like the back of his hand. He could read the greens with pinpoint precision and knew every dip, mound, and trap on the fairways. After hitting a blind shot over his head, I would make my way down the fairway to where he was standing. And often as I looked at my ball nestled safely in the middle of the short grass, I couldn't believe the potential trouble lining the course to the right and left of my ball—trouble I was able to avoid, thanks to my insightful caddy.

In spite of the terrible weather and the impending obstacles, I came away with a 69 for the day. Bob had guided me through to one of the best rounds I've ever shot, putting me well into contention for the tournament.

There's no way to overstate the importance of a good caddy during a round, especially if you're playing a course that is unfamiliar to you and filled with possibilities for trouble. A caddy often serves as your eyes and ears, watching for things you don't see and guiding you through to safety. If he is wise and insightful, you can gain a lot of knowledge by heeding his advice. And good caddies always have your best interest in mind on the course.

So pick a good caddy, and then trust him.

LET YOUR CADDY HELP

The very next day, during my second round at Pine Valley, the weather was perfect. The sun was shining, the course was dry, and the fairways were much more visible. It was a great day for scoring, and I was sure

I knew where everything was, so I felt confident I could handle things without Bob's help. I thought I knew where all the blind trouble spots were located and started trying to steer my ball away from them on my own. It didn't work as I had planned, and I came away that day with an 81.

Having the best caddy on the course won't help much if you don't utilize his services and ask for his help.

LIFE'S MOST FAITHFUL CADDY

The course of life can often get more treacherous and uncertain than most of us are able to handle on our own. When the heavy storms loom overhead and our visibility gets clouded, and we're staring down the barrel of a fairway that is dangerous and unfamiliar, we need someone there beside us who will smile and say, "Let me show you the way. I'll go ahead of you and stand in the fairway, and you just aim in my direction. I'll see that you stay safe and on the course."

> FOR THE EYES OF THE LORD RANGE THROUGHOUT THE EARTH TO STRENGTHEN THOSE WHOSE HEARTS ARE FULLY COMMITTED TO HIM.
>
> 2 CHRONICLES 16:9

That's what the writer of Hebrews meant when he wrote, "Let us fix our eyes on Jesus, the author and perfecter of our faith" (Heb. 12:2). Jesus knows this course we play like the back of his hand. He's been through it, and he knows the fear we feel and the dangers we face along the way. Wherever we go, he is standing in the fairway in the distance, beckoning us on, saying, "Just aim in this direction, and you'll be fine." And we know we can trust him—not just because he knows the course but because he always has our best interest in mind.

I remember a speech that Larry Nelson gave years ago during one of our tour Bible studies. He was talking about how to get through tough times, and he read from James 4:2: "You do not have, because you do not ask God." He explained that many times the reason we don't feel God's hand in our lives is simply because we forget to ask for his help. He is there to guide us through any circumstance we might run across, although we so often try to make it on our own.

In any situation, just aim at Jesus and you'll come out fine.

IN GOOD AND BAD TIMES

It's also important to remember that Jesus is there for us even when the weather is clear and sunny. Often when things seem to be going in our favor, we tend to think we can make it on our own. We convince ourselves that we'll be able to steer clear of danger and get through the round fine without him. We begin to rely on our own strengths and abilities and don't bother to ask for his guidance. We place our confidence in our own knowledge of the course instead of in his wisdom and insight.

In this way, we often set ourselves up for failure. Trouble comes most often when our guards are down and we think we can't get into trouble—when we begin to depend on our instincts instead of on the sound advice of a wise and trustworthy caddy.

Even in good times and clear weather, we need to fix our eyes on Jesus.

28

BE COURTEOUS TO OTHER PLAYERS

One of my best friends on the PGA tour was Bob Unger, a fellow golfing professional I was able to lead to the Lord in 1973, just a few days before we both qualified for the tour. When Bob gave his life to the Lord, he became on fire for Jesus, sharing his new faith with everyone he came into contact with. He was an inspiration to me and to many others. Just playing a practice round with him was an amazing blessing.

Bob had a custom on tour that really impressed me. When playing in a tournament, he would take every opportunity to shake the hands of the volunteers and marshals working the course and thank them for their efforts. When he saw a marshal on the side of the fairway, he'd go over and say, "I really appreciate your taking the time to volunteer out here. Thank you for your help." He'd do the same with those driving the cars or working the tents, even the kids selling drinks at the concession stands. Bob loved blessing others with kind words. He once told me how he first came to develop this habit.

It happened during a tournament at White Marsh in Philadelphia. On the first hole, a long par-3, Bob pushed his drive into the high, thick rough just right of the green. This is not where you want to be at White Marsh. The grass is so course that it's like hitting out of barbed wire. When Bob got to his ball, a marshal was standing over it, about three feet away. The ball was buried deep in the rough, and Bob

> **A BUOYANT, POSITIVE APPROACH TO THE GAME IS AS BASIC AS A SOUND SWING.**
>
> TONY LEMA

was already frustrated with his lie, but for some reason the marshal wouldn't move. He stood his ground, hovering right next to Bob during his practice swings.

Before taking his shot, Bob looked at the man and said, "Would you mind moving back a little?" The marshal glared at him, then moved back about two inches. Bob wasn't sure what the man's problem was, but he asked him again, as nicely as he could. "Would you mind moving back a little more?" The man again backed up about two inches and then planted himself firmly.

He's trying to throw me off, Bob thought to himself, though he didn't understand why. He decided to try his best to ignore the marshal and take the shot, but the distraction got to him. He duffed his chip and two-putted for a bogey.

Walking to the second hole, Bob struggled to control his anger and keep his focus intact. But the incident was still weighing on his mind, so he again pulled his tee shot, this time into the trees. Now he was really angry. But as he began the long walk down the fairway, he suddenly gained his composure and started talking to the Lord. "I know I've got to get over this anger," he prayed. "Please help me calm down and play." His frustration began to subside.

But as Bob approached the ball, he noticed another marshal standing right beside it, again about three feet away. *Not again,* he thought to himself. *Why is this happening to me?*

His initial reaction was one of anger, but he quickly caught himself and began to pray. "Dear Lord, I don't know what's going on here, but I'm not going to let it get to me. I'm sorry for my anger. I know I've just been selfish. I'm going to give this round to you. Show me what you want me to do, and I'll do it."

As Bob arrived at his ball, the marshal said to him, "It doesn't look too good. The ball is buried in some pretty thick stuff."

Bob surveyed his shot, and it looked nearly impossible. The rough was deep, and a tree limb hung down low in front of him, right in the way of his flight path. It was one of the most difficult shots he'd ever seen.

Bob looked at the man and said, "That's okay, I can hit it out."

He took out a club, then before hitting, he turned to the marshal again and said, "I want you to know how much I appreciate your being out here, sacrificing your time to help with this tournament. It really means a lot to me, and to the rest of the players."

The man looked stunned. Bob continued.

"By the way, would you mind moving back just a few feet? I really get nervous when people are standing too close."

"You bet I will," said the marshal. "I'll stand on my head if you want me to. Honestly, I've been doing this for years, and that's the first time anyone's ever said thanks to me."

The man's statement really made an impact on Bob. He suddenly understood how much he and the other players had been taking the volunteers for granted. It was an eye-opening revelation.

As the marshal stepped a good distance away from the ball, Bob thanked him, then again surveyed his shot. His only option was a low duck-hook beneath the tree, so he took a 6-iron and made his best attempt. The ball miraculously rolled up onto the green and stopped a foot shy of the pin—a tap-in for birdie.

At that moment, the Lord spoke to Bob's spirit, saying, "That's the way I want you to act on the course. Not because it will make your game better, but because I want you to demonstrate my love and kindness to others."

From that day forward, Bob committed to doing just that. And he always did.

A SIMPLE NOTE

As a young man in high school and college, I had a friend and playing partner named Lee Evans. He and I traveled and played in tournaments together. Lee had a custom that really impressed me. Whenever he would go to an event or stay in the home of a friend, he always made a habit of writing thank-you notes afterward. He carried stationery with him wherever he went and often took time to sit down and write notes

> BEING ABLE TO HELP PEOPLE AND
> GIVE BACK—THAT'S WHAT GOLF
> IS ALL ABOUT.
>
> TIGER WOODS

to people he had met during the day or to friends who had helped him in some way. God later impressed on my heart the importance of this simple act of kindness, and I began doing the same thing.

During my years on the PGA tour I started writing thank-you notes to people I stayed with, as well as to the directors of the tournaments, the volunteers, and anyone else I could think of that might be touched by a word of appreciation. For a time I made a commitment to write at least one letter a day to a friend or loved one, just to let them know I was thinking about them and praying for them. It was a wonderful experience, and I know people were touched by it, because many would write me back to let me know how much my letter meant to them and how timely my words of encouragement had been in their lives. I didn't write in order to get letters back; I just felt the need to let people know how much I appreciated their friendship. And it was humbling to see how God used those letters to touch my friends' lives.

Though I've not maintained this practice as a daily habit, I still make a point of sending short notes and letters to people often. It not only helps me keep in touch with friends, but it also serves to brighten their day. And I've found that people often enjoy returning the favor, which in turn makes them want to spend more time keeping in touch with their friends.

When I write notes to people, I consciously try to focus on them and not on myself. The temptation is usually to write and tell people about what's going on in my life, what book I'm working on, or how many golf clinics I have lined up, but I fight that urge and instead write words of encouragement and affirmation, letting them know what a blessing they are to me and my family. I've learned that because of my earlier struggles with low self-esteem and insecurity, I often find myself craving the praise of others. For years I looked to my wife and children and friends for the affirmation I never got from my earthly father, and at times that hunger caused me to want to boast of my accomplishments. I wanted to make sure these letters to others didn't turn into just another way to feed my ego, so I made a commitment early on not to let that happen. And it has proven to be a great tool not only for touching the lives of others but also for helping me focus outward instead of inward.

I hope you'll give this simple practice a try. You'll be surprised by how God will use your efforts to touch the lives of those you care for.

HARVEY PENICK'S PRAYER

Before each and every one of his teaching seminars, the late Harvey Penick would always begin by reciting this short and humble prayer:

> Dear God,
>
> We come to Thee with a prayer that the Holy Spirit will be with us for this meeting. Help us to remember that very few professions have as much influence on people as the golf pro.

Guide us and direct us in Thy way of life, that this will be a better world because we have lived in it.

Amen.[1]

The simplest acts of kindness can often be the most effective.

---

[1]Harvey Penick with Bud Shrake, *And If You Play Golf, You're My Friend* (New York: Simon and Schuster, 1993), 168.

29

DEVELOP AN ATTITUDE
OF GRATITUDE

Over the last few years I've had the privilege of playing in a lot of 40-plus tournaments. It's a competitive golf circuit that helps a number of players prepare for the Senior tour. One of the players I met on this circuit is a man named David Smith—a man of deep faith and a great golfer who has written a wonderful book on the disciplines of the game.

I was once playing a round with David at the Heathrow Country Club in Orlando, and we came to the sixteenth hole, which is a long par-5. The wind was to our backs that day, so we knew we had a chance to reach the green in two if we could push our drives far enough down the fairway. We both hit great tee shots that traveled over 300 yards toward the hole. Surveying our second shots, we both had about 250 yards to the pin. The wind was still to our backs, but the fairways sloped steeply toward the green. A lake loomed across the fairway, directly in our flight path.

To make the shots, we would need to connect perfectly with our 3-woods from a severe downhill lie and somehow get our balls to hit the green and stick—a nearly impossible shot.

We were sitting in the cart discussing this difficult task and the bad hand we'd been dealt, and I said to David, "It just doesn't seem fair to hit a ball so far and straight, right down the middle of the fairway, and still have such a hard shot into the green." David agreed with me and then stepped up to hit his shot. Standing over his ball, he took a long pause, then looked back at me and said, "You know, I'll bet there are a lot of people fighting for their lives in Bosnia who would love to have this lie."

Suddenly our game took on a new perspective. After that, our conversation began to shift in tone. Instead of complaining about our difficult shots, we began looking for reasons to be grateful.

> EVEN IF YOU AREN'T HAVING AN EXTRA GOOD DAY, ALWAYS COUNT YOUR BLESSINGS. BE THANKFUL YOU ARE ABLE TO BE OUT ON A BEAUTIFUL COURSE. MOST PEOPLE IN THE WORLD DON'T HAVE THAT OPPORTUNITY.
>
> FRED COUPLES

David and I cashed pretty good checks for the tournament that day, and we went away thanking God for the many blessings in our lives. We both went home to well-fed families and comfortable beds, and neither of us had to worry about where our next meal would be coming from. And we wouldn't be dodging bullets and mortar the next day!

I once heard it said that "the smallest package in the world is a man wrapped up in himself." It's much too easy to remain focused on the small inconveniences that come our way—to become like spoiled and ungrateful children—but we should never forget the magnitude of blessings that God has put into our lives—blessings that many in the world know nothing about. So the next time you find yourself or someone else complaining on the course, stop for a moment and try to put things in perspective.

ANOTHER SHOT OF PERSPECTIVE

I was once playing in another tournament, at the Colonial Country Club, and on the par-3 sixteenth hole I pushed my tee shot into the bunker behind the green. As I was stomping off the tee box toward the hole, muttering under my breath about my bad luck, a shimmering glint of light to one side caught my eye. It was coming from the gallery. I looked over and noticed that it was the sun reflecting off a wheelchair. A paraplegic man sat alone, watching the tournament from behind the ropes, giving me a big welcome smile as I started down the fairway.

Suddenly my shot didn't seem so bad. A giant tear started to form in my eye as I walked by him.

How sad that we so easily slip into an attitude of selfishness and ingratitude and seldom stop to look at how much we've been given.

EMBRACING GOD'S LOVE

Like many children of alcoholic fathers, I really struggled with a lot of feelings of inadequacy. During my days on tour, I constantly pushed myself to be better—often setting up unrealistic expectations for my life and my game. The pressure I put on myself was enormous and often drove me toward self-destruction and fits of anger on the course. It's a common curse for people who were never able to come to grips with their own worth due to distant and unloving fathers.

> **SOMETIMES THE BIGGEST PROBLEM IS IN YOUR HEAD.**
>
> JACK NICKLAUS

This pattern came to an all-time high for me during one particular tournament in Memphis, during the 1980 season. I was really struggling with my putter in one round. I was hitting every green in regulation and had several good chances for birdies, but I couldn't seem to get it into the cup. No matter how hard I tried to keep the ball on line, I continued to misread the greens or push it right or left. Coming into the eleventh hole, I found myself sitting at 3 over par, even though I had been putting for birdie on every hole on the course. The frustration I felt was off the scale.

A man named Jack Tobias was following me around in the gallery that day. Jack was a friend, a missionary from the Memphis area who always came to see me play when I was in town. He was a wonderful man who had given up a lucrative career to work with people in the inner city. I had tremendous respect for Jack and was consciously aware of his presence as I made my way around the course, trying desperately to hold my temper, though I was honestly on the verge of exploding.

My approach shot on the eleventh hole was a brilliant 9-iron that landed the ball within three feet of the cup—an easy putt, straight uphill. *Surely I can make this,* I thought to myself. I lined it up, took my stroke, and once again missed the cup slightly to the right. I was furious. It was all I could do to keep from burying my club into the nearest tree. I gritted my teeth and stormed toward the next hole. The rage in my face was easily apparent to the gallery and the other players, and everyone steered clear of me.

Suddenly I caught a glimpse of a figure standing behind a tree on the far side of the green. It was Jack. He was motioning with his forefinger for me to come over and talk to him. The last thing I wanted to do was to see Jack in my state of mind, but he persisted, so I walked over to where he was standing.

"What's wrong with you?" he said, with a hint of disgust in his voice.

"I'm just so frustrated," I answered. "I can't take this anymore." I was ashamed to look him in the eye.

"I thought you were a Christian, Wally," he said to me. "You're supposed to set a good example."

"I know I am," I snapped, "but it's just so hard out here." I tried desperately to keep my composure.

Jack thought for a second and then said to me, "I know what your problem is, Wally. I've followed you for the last few years, and I know something about you that you probably don't understand. I know why you let this game get to you."

He had my attention. "What is it?" I asked.

"Your problem is, you just won't let God love you."

For several seconds I sat and weighed Jack's words. The full truth of his statement didn't register in my mind at the moment, but as I moved through the final holes I began to understand what he meant. I had spent so much of my life on a performance treadmill, constantly trying to prove my worth to myself and to others, that I had never learned how to simply be content with who I am. I couldn't handle failure, because failing meant I wasn't worthy. I thought I had to give 120 percent on everything I did. I had convinced myself that the only way to be loved and accepted was to win, to be the best, to never mess up. Could God possibly love a miserable, wretched loser?

> FOR I AM CONVINCED THAT NEITHER DEATH NOR LIFE, NEITHER ANGELS NOR DEMONS, NEITHER THE PRESENT NOR THE FUTURE, NOR ANY POWERS, NEITHER HEIGHT NOR DEPTH, NOR ANYTHING ELSE IN ALL CREATION, WILL BE ABLE TO SEPARATE US FROM THE LOVE OF GOD THAT IS IN CHRIST JESUS OUR LORD.
>
> ROMANS 8:38–39

Jack's words of confrontation had a profound impact on my life. Looking back, I can see the tremendous risk he took in challenging me. I'm now deeply touched by the thought that he loved me enough to step in and intervene when he saw the dangerous path I was traveling on. Today I try to remember Jack's boldness whenever I see a friend heading for trouble, and I pray I'll have the same guts and wisdom that Jack showed that day.

After the round, Jack and I got together, and he began to minister to me. We read through a number of the psalms of David, focusing on the depth and breadth of God's love. Jack encouraged me to begin reading and meditating on the Psalms daily, especially the thirtieth through the fortieth psalms, and to learn to embrace the unconditional love that God has for us.

I took Jack's advice to heart, and over the months and years to come the Psalms became an incredible refuge for me. I began drinking in David's words, particularly his words in Psalm 37. "If the LORD delights in a man's way, he makes his steps firm; though he stumble, he will not fall, for the LORD upholds him with his hand" (Ps. 37:23–24).

Slowly I began to sense the incredible love and forgiveness of God, and as I read, I could almost feel his great loving hands encircle my heart and body. Nothing has done more to help me overcome my deep feelings of inadequacy and insecurity than learning to focus on God's love and affection. Today when I pray, I no longer dwell on my failures, begging his forgiveness; I instead thank him for accepting me as I am and for remembering my sins no more.

I've learned to simply rest in God's unconditional love and to be grateful that I no longer have to prove I am worthy of it.

30

KEEP A POSITIVE OUTLOOK

Some of my best golf on the tour occurred during my early years. At that time I enjoyed having my old college roommate come out and caddy for me. His name was Joe Prochaska (or "Joe the Pro," as we called him), and he and I always had a great time on the course together.

We developed a routine that seemed to work well for me. As we approached a tee box, the first thing we would do was to survey the course for potential problem areas. We'd look at where the OB markers were, gauge the wind and other elements, and look for hills and dips on the course that might get us into trouble. Then once we knew all of the bad things that could happen, Joe would turn to me and say, "Okay, Wally, what do you want to do?"

The minute Joe posed that question, my mind turned to focus on the positive plays. I'd pick a spot out in the fairway where I wanted to be and then tell Joe what kind of shot I planned to use to get there. We'd discuss which club I needed to pull the shot off, and then he'd reach into the bag and get it for me. Then he'd say to me, "Okay, Wally, take a practice swing and show me what you're going to do."

I'd take a few swings, and then he'd say, "That's perfect. Now tee one up and do it just like that. You can do it. This is an easy shot for you."

I was almost always able to pull it off, thanks to Joe's encouragement. Throughout our rounds together, he consistently built me up with positive thoughts and reinforcement. We remained keenly aware of the negative things that could happen, but we never allowed ourselves to dwell on them. Joe understood the importance of confidence and a positive outlook on the course. And I played some of the best golf of my life when Joe was on my bag.

> FINALLY, BROTHERS, WHATEVER IS TRUE, WHATEVER IS NOBLE, WHATEVER IS RIGHT, WHATEVER IS PURE, WHATEVER IS LOVELY, WHATEVER IS ADMIRABLE——IF ANYTHING IS EXCELLENT OR PRAISEWORTHY—— THINK ABOUT SUCH THINGS.
>
> PHILIPPIANS 4:8

In golf it's important not only to keep a good, upbeat attitude but also to surround ourselves with optimistic people—people who believe in us, even when we start to doubt ourselves and our abilities.

Nothing will destroy a person more quickly and easily than allowing negative thoughts to slip in and take hold. Losing faith in yourself and your game is a sure formula for failure—both on and off the course.

HALF EMPTY OR HALF FULL?

There are two distinct ways to look at the many traps and obstacles lining a golf course: We can view them as hazards, intent on keeping us from achieving our goal to score well, or as gentle guides leading us forward toward the hole.

The first view says that the course is out to get you, that you'd better be on your toes or else you'll find yourself in trouble, that golf is hard and cumbersome and full of bad breaks for those unlucky enough to find them—in other words, that the glass is half empty.

The other view sees that boundaries are our friends, our helpers, that the trees and bunkers and OB markers are there to point us in the right direction and lead us on to where we need to be, that without them we wouldn't know which way to aim and would have almost no chance of scoring—in other words, that the glass is half full.

Both views are correct, of course, but only the latter will help you play better golf.

SIMPLE PLEASURES

I have a vivid memory of a day when I was about thirteen years old. I was on the second hole of the Indian Lake Country Club in my hometown, Oaklandon, Indiana, walking up and down the right side of the fairway, hunting for lost balls. I wasn't playing that day; I had a higher goal in mind. I had just qualified to play in a junior tournament, and I wanted a nice, clean Titleist ball to play with. I knew that all the pros used Titleists, but on my family's tight budget, I usually had to settle for whatever was on sale at the time or for whatever I could scrounge up in the cornfields around the course. But you don't play tournaments with worn-out balls, so I was intent on finding a perfect, unblemished Titleist—just like the ones Arnie and Jack and Gary always used.

I picked out a spot on the second hole, in the field about 250 yards from the tee box, right where a good slice might end up, and I began to work the ground beside the fence, back and forth. The hole bordered a dairy farm and as I watched for balls with one eye, I had to watch for bulls with the other. I also had to be careful where I stepped.

I found a few generic balls and X-outs and tucked them into my coat pocket, but they weren't what I was looking for, so I kept searching, feeling the ground with my toes as I went.

Suddenly, there it was! A brand new Titleist—a fresh, white one that looked like it had just come out of the box. I was so excited I could hardly contain myself. Finally I was ready for the tournament. I slipped the ball into my pocket and started to leave but then decided I'd give the field one last go-through before heading

MAINTAIN A CHILDHOOD ENTHUSI-ASM FOR THE GAME OF GOLF.

CHI CHI RODRIGUEZ

home. No luck. After ten minutes I decided to call it quits. I reached into my pocket to look at the Titleist one more time, and to my utter dismay it was gone! How could I have dropped it?

Immediately I began scouring through the rough to find it again. It was getting dark and time was of the essence. I knew it couldn't be far away, and I wasn't about to go home empty-handed, especially since I knew it was there somewhere—I'd just had it in my fingers.

It took me ten more minutes to find the ball, but I finally did—buried in a deep patch I had stopped to bend over during my last search. This time I hung on to the ball tightly until I was safely home.

I'm not sure why this memory stands out so vividly in my mind. After all, it's only a golf ball, isn't it? Since that day I've easily played over ten thousand bright and shiny Titleist balls on the course, both in tournaments and in games with friends.

Perhaps it's because this story reminds me to never underestimate the simple joys and pleasures of the game. It's easy to get wrapped up in the big thrills of life, the shouts of the galleries, the shots that come out of nowhere to save the day, the course records, the big checks at the end of a tournament. We've all had moments that seem bigger than life, and they are the ones that usually dominate our memory—the ones we love to relive over dinner with friends.

Yet it is the simple pleasures that give life the most flavor and meaning. Sneaking into your son's room to slip a quarter under his pillow and retrieve a lost tooth, holding your wife's hand as you walk along the beach, watching fireworks from your deck on the Fourth of

July. These are the little things that come our way from time to time to remind us that life is good, that we are loved, that God is still on his throne.

Maybe that's why this story is stuck in my memory with such clarity.

And then again, maybe it's because I still get a thrill out of finding lost balls.

KEEP YOUR CHIN UP

On the driving range, I often notice a player standing over the ball, trying to keep their head down. The attempt usually causes the muscles in their neck to tense, which forces their chin down into their chest. This keeps the shoulders from making a full turn during the swing.

When my students are struggling with this problem, I recommend this simple drill: Address the ball and then hold up your chin. Look at the ball through the bottom of your eyes so you can see well enough to hit. As you make your swing, be careful not to let your left shoulder touch your chin on the take-away. Then follow through with the swing, keeping your chin in the air and your eyes downward. You'll be amazed how this frees your shoulders to make a full and extended turn around the spine.

I also like to use a biblical analogy to help my students remember this tip. When the Lord was preparing Gideon and his army to march on Midian, he started by commanding Gideon to sift his men before the battle. God told Gideon to take his army of ten thousand men to the lake for a drink and watch them. The ones who put their hands to their mouths and lapped the water with their tongues were to go with him into battle, but the men who got down on their hands and knees to drink were sent away. Only three hundred men passed the test. They were the ones who kept their chins up when they drank, allowing them to remain ready for battle at a second's notice. These were the men the Lord wanted by Gideon's side as he took Midian. (See Judges 7:4–8.)

This story is a good mental image to remember, both in golf and in life. Keep your chin up, and stay ready for anything. And be prepared to make a good, full turn.

Watch Your Words

The late Harvey Penick was once serving as honorary starter at the Texas Women's Amateur Championship at the Barton Creek Club course. While sitting in his cart, taking in the sights, a friend of his from Austin—a woman named Carrel— came over to say hi and give him a hug. They exchanged some polite conversation, and then Carrel stood and said, "Well, Harvey, I have to go play now."

> **Playing golf is a privilege, not a sentence.**
>
> Harvey Penick

Harvey caught her by the hand and pulled her back, then said to her, "Carrel, you don't *have* to go play. You *get* to go play. There's a world of difference."

"You're right," she said, smiling at him.

From that day on, Carrel always watched her words when talking to Harvey.

THE PERFECT GOLFER

His drives are rather ragged and his iron shots are punk;
His putting's an amazing thing; he's rarely ever sunk,
A putt much longer than a foot; his mashie stroke's a sin;
Somehow he cannot seem to get a touch of Hagen spin
To hold it safely on the green; his brassie shot's the type
The devil teaches when the lads are slightly under-ripe.

And more than that he knows all traps; not one but has its
charms
And welcomes him with encores and, it seems, with out-
stretched arms;
But somehow it can't feaze him much; a song is in his heart
And on his lips a whistle and a jest of golfing art.
When he comes in he always has the graciousness to say
"This Club is perfect, I have had a most delightful day."
And though we jest and laugh at him, we'll tell the wide
world flat
"God made the golf course brighter when he made a man
like that."

John E. Baxter, *Locker Room Ballads*

31

COUNT EVERY STROKE

I n one of my previous books, I asked my friend Tim LaHaye—a highly respected author and theologian—if he would honor me by writing the introduction. He gracefully agreed and submitted a wonderful writing that included the following excerpt about a man he used to play golf with.

> The man who first introduced me to golf was a fellow minister-friend with whom I had gone to school. Whenever we played, he volunteered to keep score, but after a few rounds, it dawned on me that he always got the lowest score in our foursome of pastors.
>
> One day we came to a small lake, and rather than take a penalty and move on if we went into the drink, he challenged us to hit until we got one on the other side. Believe it or not, all three of us hit our first drive safely to the other side, putting enormous pres-

THE ONLY WAY OF REALLY FINDING OUT A MAN'S TRUE CHARACTER IS TO PLAY GOLF WITH HIM.

P. G. WODEHOUSE

sure on him. It took him seven balls to get across. Later I noticed that he only counted two of those water balls.

One time he had 3 balls going at the same time and claimed the one with the lowest score was his "official" ball. Other times, instead of counting short putts, he just picked up his ball and said, "That's a gimme." Finally, I got up enough nerve to suggest that his best club was his pencil, which was why he always got the lowest score.

Over time, I have noticed that anyone who cheats in golf has a tendency to cheat in life. My friend was no exception. Of the four of us, this man was decidedly the best preacher, and the most highly respected in his denomination. Yet, the truth is, he was a cheat! He cheated in golf, and he cheated in life. He cheated on his wife, his church, his Lord, and his family. Today he is a hollow shell of what he could have been.[1]

PLAY IT AS IT LIES

Jack Nicklaus once said, "If there's one thing golf demands above all else, it's honesty." By its very nature, golf is a game of honor and integrity. It takes a lot of character for a man to stand alone in a patch of deep rough, with a pitiful lie beneath his ball and no one else in sight, and hit it as it lies. Or to make the long walk back to the tee after seeing that the ball has landed about an inch out of bounds between two white stakes. The temptation to prop the ball up a bit with a club is more than a lot of golfers can handle, so we often chalk it up in our minds to winter rules and make the adjustment. But that kind of habit isn't good for your game or for your character.

The true character of any man is measured by what he does when he is all alone—when no one else is looking. Dave Hill once said, "Golf is the hardest game in the world to play and the easiest to cheat

---

[1]Tim LaHaye, introduction to *Finishing the Course,* by Jim Sheard and Wally Armstrong (Nashville: J. Countryman, 2000), 9–10.

at." Given that truth, it seems appropriate to me that when we step up to the tee box, the first question asked is, "Who has the honor?" Even the language of golf demands an honest approach.

It's interesting to note that the mulligan was never intended to have a place in the old game of golf. It was, in fact, invented by a duffer in America, some time after the game came to the United States.

> **ONCE YOU GIVE UP YOUR ETHICS, THE REST IS A PIECE OF CAKE.**
>
> J. R. EWING
> (FROM THE TV SERIES *DALLAS*)

The rules of golf are clear. Wherever your ball happens to end up, if it's in bounds, you're expected to play it as it lies. You would expect the same from your opponent, so hold yourself to it, as well. It will make you a better golfer, and a better person.

A SHINING EXAMPLE

When golfers talk about honesty on the course, the name of Tom Kite almost always comes up. More than most, Tom Kite has shown himself to be a man of tremendous integrity, both in golf and in life.

Even during his earliest days on tour, Kite quickly became known as a man that could be trusted completely. During one tournament about twenty years ago, he was coming down the homestretch tied for the lead. On one shot he inadvertently brushed the ball with the tip of his club, and without hesitation, he walked over to one of the officials and reported the violation, costing himself a stroke. No one had seen the infraction, and he could have easily gotten away with it, but he didn't. Instead, he chose to do the right thing. He finished the tournament in second place, just one stroke off the lead, and afterward reporters scrambled to his side to ask why he would call a violation on himself and throw away the tournament. His simple answer was, "There is only one way to play the game."

Those who know Tom understand that the foundation beneath his amazing integrity is his faith in God. Tom knew that God had seen his mistake even if no one else had, and his relationship with his Lord was much too precious a thing to take for granted. When given the choice between winning a tournament and keeping his integrity intact, Tom chose the higher road. And through the years, God has been glorified every time this story has been told or remembered.

During another tournament years later—the 1993 Kemper Open—Tom Kite was leading the pack and was paired with Grant Waite of New Zealand during the third round. On the fourth hole, Waite took a drop from a ground under repair area, and as he was preparing to hit, Kite noticed that Waite's heel was slightly outside the OB marker. It would have been easy for Kite to look away and hope that an official would notice the infraction and give Waite a two-shot penalty, but instead Kite quickly stopped his opponent and pointed to his heel. "We don't need any penalties here," Tom said to him.

> IN FOOTBALL AND HOCKEY YOU COME INTO INTIMATE—AND OFTEN FORCIBLE ENOUGH—CONTACT WITH THE OUTER MAN; CHESS IS A CLASH OF INTELLECTS; BUT IN GOLF CHARACTER IS LAID BARE TO CHARACTER.
>
> ARNOLD HAULTAIN

The grateful Grant Waite changed his stance before making a beautiful approach shot into the green.

Waite won the tournament by one stroke, and Kite again came in second. Once more the reporters gathered around to ask Kite if he had any doubts about his decision to intervene. He told them, "It would be pretty chicken for me to stand by and watch a guy accidentally break a rule and then say, 'By the way, add two strokes.' That's not golf. That's other sports where guys are trying to get every advantage they can."

A true man of God knows that honesty and honor are the only true paths to greatness, both in golf and in life.

32

DON'T FORGET
TO HAVE FUN

I mentioned earlier that during my early years on the tour I often called my old college roommate, "Joe the Pro," to caddy for me. He and I always had a great time on the course. He initially thought caddying would be a piece of cake—just a handful of guys walking around the fairways, shooting the breeze. But he soon discovered it actually involves a lot of skill and work.

Before I met him, Joe didn't have much of a golfing background. He knew the basic rules, but he was often lost when it came to game etiquette or the fundamental courtesies of the course. As a result, a lot of the other players didn't quite know how to handle him. Joe was also something of a cutup, and it spilled out onto the course. I liked his attitude, because it kept me from taking myself too seriously, but his antics didn't always go over well with others, especially the other caddies on tour.

I remember playing in a tournament at Westchester in Rye, New York, with Joe on my bag. We were paired with Hubert Green and his long-time veteran caddy of ten years, a man named Shane. They'd won a lot of tournaments through the years, including the U.S. Open, and Shane took his role very seriously.

Joe and I attended the University of Florida, and we were both rabid Gator fans. Joe knew that Hubert was an avid fan of Florida State—a Seminole—so around the second tee Joe started ragging on him. Joe continued to make comments to Hubert as we made our way down the course toward the third hole, taunting him about how badly the Gators were going to beat the 'Noles that season.

THE GAME IS MEANT TO BE FUN.

JACK NICKLAUS

It's kind of a given in golf that caddies are not supposed to bother the players during a round, but Joe didn't understand this courtesy. Had I known that Joe was bothering Hubert, I would have stepped in and stopped him, but I was so busy focusing on my own game that I didn't even notice.

On the third tee box, Shane grabbed Joe by the shirt and said, "Look, Hubert's not interested in hearing about the Gators. He's here to win a tournament."

Joe got the message and backed off for a while.

Coming into the seventeenth hole, Hubert was one shot off the lead. We hit our tee shots, and then while making our way down the fairway, Shane came over to me and said angrily, "You'd better do something about your caddy. If he bothers Hubert one more time, I'm going to punch his lights out."

I had no idea what he was talking about, so I asked Joe what had been going on. He laughed and said he'd just been having some fun with Hubert.

"What did you do to make Shane so mad?" I asked him.

He said, "Back on the sixth hole he was walking around with his chest stuck out, so I asked him, 'Does this prancing around like a pea-cock come naturally to you, or do you have to work at it?' He's been mad at me ever since. And I guess he doesn't like it when I talk to Hubert."

Suddenly I understood why Shane wasn't too amused.

The interesting thing was, Hubert didn't seem bothered by any of Joe's antics. In fact, I think one of the reasons Hubert had been playing so well was because Joe's sense of humor loosened him up. But I decided I'd better keep my eye on things through the next few holes.

Hubert's second shot on seventeen went over the green and nestled into the rough for an almost impossible lie. My shot left me a long putt for birdie. Then Hubert hit an incredible pitch shot to within six inches of the hole. It was a brilliant recovery. Shane stood on the edge of the green, holding the flag and grinning from ear to ear.

While lining up my putt, I looked over to see Joe slowly sneaking up behind him. *Oh, no! What's he going to do now?* I thought to myself. Joe startled Shane by stepping up in front of him and then said something to him that no one could hear. For a few seconds they just stood looking at each other, and then suddenly Shane began to laugh out loud. They shook hands and we finished the hole. Hubert ended the day one shot off the lead.

When I asked Joe later what he had said to Shane, he told me, "I just told him that even though it's been a tough day, I wanted to make sure we were still best buddies." That totally disarmed Shane and erased any anger he might have had. After the round the two of them went out for drinks together.

Golf is a serious enough sport without our adding even more pressure on the course. The best approach to a round is usually to keep it light and to remember to have fun. To a lot of us, golf may be a business, but it's still just a game.

SAY WHAT?

One of the first times Joe caddied for me was during a pro-am at White Marsh, an old course located just outside of Philadelphia.

While standing on the first tee, one of the players asked, "How far is it to the pin?"

Joe took a good look down the fairway and said, "Looks like about a block and a half."

The funniest part is, he wasn't joking.

ONE MORE JOE STORY

Of all the times I thought Joe was going to get me into trouble, the one that truly takes the cake was during a tournament at White Marsh when I was paired with Jerry Pate. Jerry had recently won the U.S. Open and was at the top of his game. We both started the tournament toward the top of the leader board, and he really had his game face on that day. I hoped and prayed that Joe would leave him alone and let him play, especially since I knew that Jerry was a big Alabama fan.

> ALWAYS KEEP IT FUN. IF YOU DON'T HAVE FUN, YOU'LL NEVER GROW AS A PERSON OR A PLAYER.
>
> TIGER WOODS

As always, Joe couldn't stop talking about the Gators, and I could tell Jerry was getting a bit irritated. On the third hole, which is a really long par-3, we both pulled our shots a bit. Jerry was on the edge of the green, and I was in the bunker behind him. I hit a great sand shot to within four feet of the cup, and as Jerry was lining up to take his shot, I noticed Joe standing in the bunker raking the trap, totally oblivious to the fact that Jerry was about to putt. Jerry stood away from his putt and looked over at me, as if to say, "Where'd you get this guy?"

I went over and told Joe to get out of the trap and stand still until Jerry had finished his shot. Jerry ran his putt ten feet past the hole and then looked at me with disgust, like it was my fault. Then he ran his next putt four feet past the hole coming back. He was as hot as I'd ever seen him, and I prayed that he would make his next one and not end up four-putting. Thankfully, he nailed it.

I was terribly embarrassed about the whole thing, but Joe didn't seem bothered in the least.

The fourth hole was a long par-4 that ran uphill, and behind the green was the ninth tee box. As I made my way over to the fourth tee box, I was thinking about what I could say to Jerry to apologize for Joe's behavior, but just as we reached the tee, I looked around and Joe was nowhere in sight. Finally Jerry and I looked over, and there was Joe, standing on the ninth tee box with my bag, without a soul around him. Jerry looked at me in disbelief. I could tell he was thinking, "This guy doesn't even know where the holes are!"

I was so embarrassed that I didn't even bother to try and explain. Joe's antics continued for the rest of the round, but fortunately Jerry was able to overlook them and concentrate on his game. Coming into the eighteenth hole, Jerry was one stroke off the lead and playing well. He hit his tee shot right down the middle, and I ended up in the trees. His second shot rolled to within ten feet of the pin on the backside. I hit mine over the trees to the front part of the green, and by the time I reached my ball, Jerry had already marked his and was squatting on the fringe, lining up his putt.

Joe and I didn't know this, so Joe walked over to take the flag out of the hole. Jerry said something to him under his breath, and Joe began walking toward him to see what he wanted. "What's wrong?" Joe asked him.

Jerry's face was red with anger. "Not only did you step on my line, but now you're walking right up it!" he scowled.

Then Jerry looked back over at me, to see what I was going to do about it.

I walked over and said, "Joe, you need to get off the green. Why don't you give Jerry's caddy the flag and go wait for me inside the scoring tent?"

As Joe walked off the green, I looked at Jerry and said, "I'm really sorry about Joe. I feel really bad about how he's been acting."

While I was lining my putt up, I glanced past the hole toward the bleachers. Some sort of movement had caught my eye and I was try-ing to see what it was. Once again, it was Joe. Through the space between a spectator's legs, I could see him squat-ting down behind the bleachers, peer-ing at me through the small opening between the seats. A big grin was on his face. I didn't know whether to laugh or cry. I two-putted, then stood back and prayed that Jerry would be able to relax and make his putt.

> ENJOY THE GAME. HAPPY GOLF
> IS GOOD GOLF.
>
> GARY PLAYER

Somehow Jerry was able to pull himself together and concentrate on his putt. He landed it in the cup to tie for the lead. I thought to myself, *Thank goodness this round is over!*

Afterward we all made our way into the scoring tent. I signed Jerry's card and, while sliding it over to him, looked over to see Joe standing right over Jerry's shoulder. I almost panicked. Jerry looked at him and said, "You again? What do you want now?"

Joe said, "I was just wondering if you had a caddy lined up for next week."

Jerry burst out laughing. I think it was the funniest thing he'd ever heard. Thankfully, he was in a good enough mood after tying for the lead to forgive Joe, and we all walked away still friends.

HOGAN SHOCKS THE GALLERY

Ben Hogan was once paired in a charity match with Morris Williams Jr., Ed Hopkins, and Harvey Penick. Hogan was known as a man who loved to drink, but he had never been known to show up on the course under the influence. You can imagine the gallery's reaction when Hogan showed up late to the first tee box, staggering, with a silly grin on his face and his cap on sideways.

All through the crowd, people could be heard whispering, "What's wrong with Hogan?" It seemed obvious to everyone that he was drunk.

As he stepped up to shoot, his knees buckled while he was trying to put the ball on the tee, and he fell over. He struggled to his feet and then staggered to and fro while standing over the ball with his club. His first attempt missed the ball altogether. The crowd gasped at the sight of the great Ben Hogan whiffing his tee shot.

> **GOLF IS A GREAT AND GLORIOUS GAME. EVEN THOSE OF US WHO EARN OUR LIVINGS AT IT PLAY IT MORE FOR THE PLEASURE THAN FOR THE MONEY.**
>
> ARNOLD PALMER

He grunted and accidentally knocked the ball backward off the tee. His caddy replaced it, and he took another swing. This time he topped the ball about fifty yards down the fairway. His playing partners hit perfect drives and then followed Hogan to his ball as the gallery followed. With his cap still sitting sideways on his head, he gave a mighty swing and sliced the ball toward the hole, but far off the fairway. The swing knocked his hat off, and his caddy quickly put it back on.

After several more shots, Hogan made it to the green. On his first putt he knocked the ball twenty feet past the hole. His second putt did the same thing, only in the opposite direction. He staggered toward the ball and hit again, but somehow this one landed right in the center of the cup. Hogan fell down trying to retrieve the ball from the hole. No one could believe what they had just witnessed.

Suddenly Hogan jumped to his feet, straightened his hat, and said to his playing partner in clear English, "Okay pardner, it's up to you on this hole. I'll do it better from now on." At that instant, the gallery and the other players caught on, and a roar of laughter went up into the air. He wasn't drunk; he was simply entertaining the crowd.

Hogan had always been such a stern competitor that no one could imagine him as the course clown. But those who knew him well remember that off the course, he always had a great sense of humor. And obviously his acting skills weren't bad either. Not one person on the course that day caught on to his little joke.

PART 6

GIVING BACK TO THE GAME

*In golf, as in life, you get out of it
what you put into it.*
SAM SNEAD

*The score is important, of course. And the
discovery that you are superior to another
golfer is satisfying. But when your score is bad
and the other fellow beats you, golf still has
been a blessing to you. The score isn't the
"be all and end all."*
TOMMY ARMOUR

*I can sum it up like this:
Thank God for the game of golf.*
ARNOLD PALMER

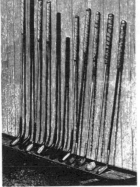

33

DEVELOP A LOVE FOR THE GAME

B en Hogan had a huge impact on me as a golfer, long before I ever met him. As a child, I used to marvel at his ability with a golf club and the level of greatness he brought to the game. I had always been a student of golf history, and Hogan was one of the few living legends of our time, so I always dreamed about getting to meet him someday. That chance finally came while I was playing at the Colonial Country Club in Fort Worth, Texas.

I was playing in a pro-am with Randall Reiley, a local federal judge. During our conversation, Randall happened to mention that he lived on the Shady Oaks course, where Hogan went every day to hit balls. In fact, the back of Randall's house overlooked the very spot where Hogan always practiced, a hole on the par-3 course nestled within the confines of the regular course. Every day Hogan practiced on that hole, right across from Randall's house, hitting hundreds of balls to his caddy, who stood by with a shag bag.

The judge invited me to come over one afternoon to watch Hogan practice, and I quickly agreed. It turned out to be one of the greatest thrills of my life. The judge wasn't able to join me on this particular day, but a friend of his named Kermit Zarley went with me. Kermit had met Hogan a few times and promised to introduce me. In fact, he told me to bring my clubs along, just in case.

I'd heard so many stories about Hogan's serious, competitive side that I was a bit apprehensive. Hogan is often depicted as a cold and hard man on the course, and during the heat of competition, he was. To my delight and surprise, however, Hogan greeted us with a warm smile and a friendly handshake. I found him to be one of the most gentle and pleasant men I had ever met. As we stood visiting on the tee box, I was struck most by the gleam in his eye as he talked about golf. After an entire life on the course, practicing and playing tournaments almost every day, he still had a deep and abiding love for the game, as well as for other pros.

THE GAME IS THE THING—NOT GAMESMANSHIP.

NANCY LOPEZ

As we talked, Hogan hit shot after shot to his caddy down the fairway, each time landing the ball with arrowlike precision. He would demonstrate shots he had been practicing recently, and you could see his eyes light up each time he took a stroke and pulled off the shot he was trying. He'd hit a high draw, then a low hook, then a fade—each one flying exactly as he had planned.

After a while, Hogan noticed that Kermit and I had our clubs with us, so he said, "Why don't you boys hit some balls?"

Looking back, the whole episode seems almost surreal to me. The fact that I was standing on a tee box trading shots with the great Ben Hogan was more of a thrill than I ever imagined I could hope for. After a while he even walked over and began encouraging us as we hit balls toward the pin. It made me nervous to think that Ben Hogan himself was standing over me, watching my swing on the course. But he couldn't have been any nicer about it.

Before that day, I had been an admirer of Hogan's swing and his competitiveness on the course. I was in awe of what he had done for the history of the game. But I've since come to see him as much, much more. He was great not just because he played great but because he epitomized everything that is right and noble about the game. Hogan was not driven by trophies or money or fame but by a deep desire to master a sport he dearly loved. It was the thrill of the game that brought him back day after day.

> **THE THING I'M MOST PROUDEST OF IS THAT I GOT BETTER EVERY DAY.**
>
> BEN HOGAN

Seeing a man who had long since quit playing tournament golf still love the game enough to come out every day and practice was a great inspiration. Hogan was a living testament to the fact that golf is a game that can bring joy to our lives long into our later years. It takes so little to give back to the game that has given us so much happiness.

Of all the things I've done and seen in my career, my afternoon hitting balls with Ben Hogan is what I treasure most. Just being near him, seeing the sparkle in his eyes, gave me a renewed love and appreciation for the greatest game on earth.

A RECORD TO BE PROUD OF

Mac O'Grady holds a golfing record not a lot of players would be proud of, but I think he should see it as a badge of honor. He holds the record for the most attempts made at qualifying school before earning a spot on the tour. From 1971 to 1981, O'Grady made sixteen tries at qualifying school before finally getting his card in 1982, on his seventeenth attempt. (From 1975 through 1981, the school was held twice a year).

Until he was able to finally make his way on tour, O'Grady did anything he had to do to support himself and his family. He worked as a cook, a busboy, a dishwasher, a caddy; he even drove a hearse for a funeral home. Most men might have given up after a few years and gone on to pursue another career, but not O'Grady. He continued to try, even when it looked as though he might never make it.

The fire that burned in O'Grady's heart and kept him going was his deep love for the game. He couldn't imagine a life without golf, so he never gave up trying. His persistence finally paid off for him.

I had the privilege of being able to play alongside Mac during the last round of qualification in 1982 as he finally gained his card. We were playing at the TPC Stadium course in Jacksonville—one of the toughest courses around. We both were playing well that day, and going into the eighteenth hole, it suddenly hit Mac that he was just one hole away from gaining his card. We each had a nice cushion, and it looked like we were home free. Then on the eighteenth, Mac hit one of the worst drives I've ever seen.

A lake was on the left side of the hole, so Mac aimed a bit right to make sure he didn't hit into it. His ball went about 150 yards dead right, ending on the far side of the sixteenth fairway. I could see the frustration in his eyes, but he was determined to recover. He hit his second shot back into the fairway and then mis-hit his third shot short of the green. He was so nervous that he shanked his fourth shot right into a deep bunker, leaving himself a nearly impossible shot to a pin nestled at the back part of the green, with water just eight feet on the other side.

Somehow Mac pulled himself together and was able to blast it out of the sand to within one foot of the hole, where he tapped in for a double bogey. It was probably the greatest pressure shot of his career.

Mac made the cut that year by one stroke. If he had not been able to recover from the bunker, he would have been looking at another year of qualifying school. Instead he went on to make a respectable name for himself on the tour. He was able to accumulate just over $1 million in earnings during his short time on the PGA circuit before he was forced to step aside because of injuries.

MEETING BYRON NELSON

During my high school and college days, I did everything I could to just be near the game of golf. I loved hanging around the top players of the day, hearing their stories and watching them play. I found that the best way to do that was to become a caddy, so I often volunteered to carry bags at the Indianapolis 500 tournament whenever it came to my hometown in Indiana. It was the next best thing to actually playing.

During my senior year of college, I was able to caddy in the Byron Nelson Classic at the Preston Trail Club, in Dallas, Texas. It was Nelson's first year to host the tournament that bears his name, and a lot of big players had signed up to be there in honor of him. I was there to caddy for Dave Regan, a fellow Gator and a tour professional. I had just finished caddying for Dave in North Carolina, and then I hitchhiked all the way to New Orleans, where I caught a short, cheap flight over to Dallas. I flew in with my tour-size University of Florida golf bag and a suitcase and wandered the airport looking for a ride to the golf course.

> I REMEMBER PLAYING MY FIRST PRACTICE ROUND WITH JoANNE CARNER AND I COULD BARELY BREATHE. AND I WAS A PROFESSIONAL!
>
> MEG MALLON

I finally caught a ride with another rookie player from Canada, and he convinced me to ride with him in the courtesy car and act like I was one of the players. That in itself was a big thrill for a young tour wanna-be.

Just as we pulled up in front of the clubhouse, Dave Regan came around the corner to greet us. As soon as he saw me, he said, "Hey, Wally, let's go in and have lunch." We went into the clubhouse and standing in the entrance was the great Byron Nelson himself. He had been working with Dave's swing, and as Dave introduced me to Nelson, he immediately invited us to have lunch with him. Of course we agreed, and as we went into the dinning room, Chris Shenkel came by to join us. Sitting at the very next table was Arnold Palmer, bigger than life.

I watched the porter carry my bags into the clubhouse, and I began to get really concerned that someone would find out I wasn't really a player. Caddies were not allowed in the clubhouse, and a caddy having lunch with the players was unheard of. But I was already in too deep to back out, so I just tried to keep my mouth shut and hope no one would notice me.

I'll never forget how great it felt to be sitting in the company of these living legends, listening to their stories over the lunch table. This is the kind of thing that every young player dreams of when he lies awake at night, and here I was experiencing it firsthand. It made an indelible impact on my life and career and gave me even more reason to want to work hard and make it onto the tour as a player.

Halfway through the lunch, Gary Player came by and told Dave and I that his caddy was ill, and he asked me if I wanted to caddy for him. I had met Gary a week earlier at a tour Bible study in North Carolina, and while there, Dave had told him that if he ever needed a good caddy, I'd be the guy to ask. Gary remembered that meeting and saw this as a chance to follow through on that offer. Dave was kind enough to let me caddy for Gary, and I worked for him for the next three weeks, at Dallas, Houston, and New Orleans.

Byron Nelson was a delightful man to meet and befriend. He was just as I had imagined him, polite and friendly—a godly man, both on and off the course. Though he had long since retired from playing, he had spent much of his life giving back to the game and helping others any way he could, always ready to pass on his love for golf to younger players. He worked with a number of players on tour, encouraging them and helping with their game whenever he could. Tom Watson often asked Byron to watch him practice and give him pointers, and so did Dave Regan and many others. Byron did the same for me six years later, when I finally gained my tour card and was able to come back in through the front door of the clubhouse—this time as a real player instead of an imposter.

More than most, Byron Nelson remains an amazing example to others of what the game of golf is all about. Even today, some thirty-two years later, Nelson still graciously welcomes players at his tournament. Moreover, the whole purpose of his tournament is to raise funds for young children. He reminds us all that no matter where we are in life, we have an obligation to reach out and encourage those who are following in our footsteps.

One of the things that make golf such a great sport is the feeling of camaraderie and respect players have for each other. Golf is a game that loves and cherishes its heroes, and it never forgets those who have made it the sport it is—a sport rich in history and sentiment, with no shortage of legends.

We golfers love the great players of our sport almost as much as we love the game itself. And that makes it a sport like no other.

34

PASS ON YOUR
PASSION

During most of the years that I played on tour, I often used local caddies from the courses where the tournaments were being played. A lot of guys on tour used the same caddy for all their games, but I liked getting to know the young players around the country.

When I was a kid, I worked my way up to become the number one caddy at the Highland Country Club in Indianapolis, Indiana. I always seemed to be able to caddy for the best players, and it meant a lot to me to be able to work with them. I got to see a lot of great golf during those years. Most of the players were very encouraging to us as we made our way around the course. That's where I first developed a deep love for the game and the people who play it. And when I finally made it on tour, I saw it as my chance to give back a little of the encouragement I had been given as a boy.

During my career, the people who ran the Western Open understood the importance of encouraging the younger generation of golfers and made a rule that anyone who played in the tournament had to use a caddy from the area. It was a great idea, even though some of the players didn't like it.

The young men and women they brought out to caddy for us were exceptional people. They were high school kids from the area, the best caddies from all the country clubs in the Chicago area. Many were in line to go to college on an Evans Scholarship—a program set up to help the most outstanding caddies with their education. These kids were the cream of the crop from the Chicago area. It was a great tradition that has since given way to big bucks and pros with egos. It's sad the organizers don't still hold to this wonderful tradition.

> THE ARDENT GOLFER WOULD PLAY MOUNT EVEREST IF SOMEBODY WOULD PUT A FLAGSTICK ON TOP.
>
> PETE DYE

The Western Open was one of my favorite tournaments to play, mostly because I so enjoyed getting to know these bright, young players. They loved the game as much as I did, and there was nothing I enjoyed more than getting together with them on the course or in the clubhouse and telling great golf stories. You could see in their eyes how much it meant to them when we included them in our activities. I understood, because I felt the same way when I was a young caddy and players showed me the same kindness.

Today I still keep in touch with a few of my past caddies from that event. Many of them are now doctors, lawyers, or schoolteachers, but I'm willing to bet that every one of them is still a golfer. Once you've been bitten by the golf bug, you seldom lose your zeal for the game.

Golf is always more satisfying when you're able to share it with others. My advice to anyone who loves the game is to look for opportunities to pass on your passion, especially to the younger generations. There is no better way to keep the history of golf alive and fresh.

CATCHING SAM SNEAD'S PASSION

During my rookie year on tour, 1974, one of the first tournaments I got to play was the World Open at Pinehurst. It was an eight-round marathon of golf on four different courses, and a lot of the old players were there to compete. Over two hundred men from around the world showed up to play.

My wife, Debbie, was as thrilled to be there as I was, and during the first two rounds of play I kept looking up to find her. I assumed she'd be watching me. I later found out she'd been following along with Arnold Palmer's gallery ("Arnie's Army"). It didn't bother me; if I hadn't been playing, that's where I would have been too.

WHAT YOU HAVE TO REMEMBER IS THAT GOLF IS A GAME THAT YOU CAN PLAY ALMOST FOREVER. IN OTHER SPORTS, A 40-YEAR-OLD ATHLETE IS AN OLD MAN.

CURTIS STRANGE

On the third day of the tournament I got my pairing sheet and found that I would be playing with the great Sam Snead on the famous number two course. What an amazing honor and privilege! I'll never forget the thrill of playing with this living legend. His strength and flexibility were something to behold—even though he was well into his senior years.

I'd heard stories of how Snead still worked to retain his flexibility. Even in his sixties and seventies, he would stand flat on the ground and try to kick the top of a door with his foot. Every day he would stretch and work out to keep his edge and stay in shape. And you could certainly see that in his swing as he crushed the ball a country mile on each hole.

Like most legends of the game, Snead was tremendously competitive and gave it his all throughout every hole. We had a great time trading shots and stories on the course. From the first tee box, it was apparent he hadn't lost his competitive edge and his desire to win. He played every shot as if he were on his way to win the U.S. Open, and his drive and passion flowed through to the rest of us. Just playing alongside him served to inspire me and push me to play better—to be the best I could possibly be.

The last time I saw Sam Snead at an event was at the Southern Open in Columbus, Georgia. He was hitting balls on the practice range, surrounded by a bunch of younger players, and I quickly grabbed my clubs and a bucket of balls to hit near him, hoping to overhear what he was saying. What I remember most about that practice

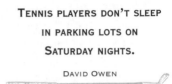

TENNIS PLAYERS DON'T SLEEP IN PARKING LOTS ON SATURDAY NIGHTS.

DAVID OWEN

range was that it was long and downhill, with a twenty-foot-high fence about 250 yards down the range. The fence was there to catch the balls on their first and second bounce. To make it over the fence, your ball would have to carry at least 260 or 270 yards. Many players couldn't do it.

It was quite a sight to see the aging Snead challenging a bunch of flatbellies to see who could carry that fence. He would crush his balls one after the other and sail them safely over to the other side, while the young, strong players would swing for all they were worth to try and keep up with him. Few could. It was a wonderful afternoon of competition, and I could tell that Snead was getting a kick out of it. It was probably the highlight of his week. Snead loved to show off his powerful swing.

One of the greatest aspects of golf is the way it brings generations together. Young players are able to play right alongside the older ones, catching their love and enthusiasm for the game, getting advice and pointers, and learning about the rich history of the sport from the very ones who made that history. You'd be hard pressed to find that dynamic on a basketball court, or a football field, or even a baseball diamond. But golf is a great equalizer, a game of skill, finesse, and experience.

More than any other game, golf is played better when caught instead of taught.

PASSING ON YOUR FAITH

Through my writing and speaking ministry, I get the chance to travel the country and talk to a lot of great young men and women. I speak at a number of Fellowship of Christian Athletes gatherings, summer junior golf camps, Christian businessmen's luncheons, and golfing events. These engagements are the highlight of my life at present.

There's nothing more encouraging than meeting young people with a deep love for God and his Word—young people with a passion for growing in their faith. Though they love hearing some of the great golf stories—almost as much as I love telling them—they're much more interested in hearing the testimonies of faith and integrity in the game, stories of people who have used their platform as a celebrity or athlete to further God's kingdom and shine the Lord's light to the world—players like Tom Lehman, Scott Simpson, Paul Azinger, and the late Payne Stewart. Instead of using their highly visible careers for personal gain, these players choose to let God work through them to reach a generation of young fans and players. Many of these men give a great deal of their time and resources to ministries and charities around the world and look for every opportunity to be a witness for Christ. Every time the TV cameras and microphones are turned on them, they see it as an opportunity to share their faith and spread God's love to others.

To me, that's the true sign of greatness—both in golf and in life. It's not about how many tournaments you've won or how much money you've made; it's about how many people were touched along the way by your life and words.

35

MENTOR YOUNGER PLAYERS

A number of years ago I got the chance to take my fourteen-year-old son, Blake, with me to watch the Masters tournament. When Blake was born I was no longer on the tour full-time, and he had never had an opportunity to see me play professionally. But he had spent many an hour over the dinner table listening to stories of the courses I had played and the people I had played with, and it was a thrill to finally be able to share a piece of my past with him. Blake had always especially loved the stories of Gary Player and couldn't wait to meet him.

As we stood along the ropes of the seventh tee box, I retold some of the old tales of my days on the tour. I was busy telling Blake again about the time I once pitched in for birdie on the sixth hole on Saturday of the Masters. Blake's eyes grew wide as I shared the account from the very place at which it had happened.

Suddenly we looked up and saw Gary Player making his way to the tee box. At that moment it hit me that it had been over twenty years since I had stood with Gary during a practice round on this very tee box. He still looked so young and fit I found it hard to believe.

Gary saw me in the gallery and had a few minutes to kill, so he made his way over to say hello. He shook Blake's hand and we reminisced a bit. Then he turned to Blake and told him of the time I had ruined his rain gear and stunk up his bag. Blake listened with excitement, though I knew he had heard the story hundreds of times before.

It happened in 1968 when I was caddying for Gary during the Houston Open.

I had slipped a few bananas into Gary's bag as a quick snack for us on the course. I then forgot the bananas were in there, and a week later, while playing in New Orleans, a downpour erupted on the course. Gary said to me, "Reach into my bag and get me my rain gear and a clean glove."

I stuck my hand into the pocket of his bag and heard a loud squishing sound. Even Gary heard it. I pulled out a mass of rubber covered in black gook. The smell was atrocious, and everyone near me took a few steps back to gasp for air. I tried my best to separate the glove from the slicker, frantically wiping off the rotting bananas, but to no avail. Gary was forced to play the rest of the round drenched and struggling to hold on to his club with a wet glove.

At the time I had felt like an idiot, but it was good to see that Gary could look back on it and laugh. And I loved seeing Blake's eyes light up as he listened to the tale again, this time from the great Gary Player himself.

Of all the joys I've been blessed to experience during my career in golf, none compare to the thrill I get from sharing my passion for

> I WISH EVERY GOLFER COULD HAVE THE KIND OF GOLFING EDUCATION I HAD. I WISH EVERY CHILD COULD HAVE THE KIND OF FATHER I HAD. IF SOMEONE COULD GRANT ME THOSE WISHES, THE WORLD WOULD BE A BETTER PLACE, AND SCORING AVERAGES WOULD BE A LOT LOWER, TOO.
>
> DAVIS LOVE III

the game with my children. There's nothing greater than getting to bring your kids into the sport, teaching them the mechanics and nuances of the swing, working with them on the range and on the course, sharing the rich history of the game with the people you love the most.

One of the great gifts God has given me is the opportunity to spend time on the course with my kids, allowing me the chance to mentor them both in golf and in life.

I encourage you to do the same. Use your love of the game to draw closer to the ones you love the most and create a bond that will never be broken.

WHEN YOUR MENTOR MENTORS

During that same trip to watch the Masters tournament, Blake and I had the opportunity to attend a Fellowship of Christian Athletes prayer breakfast for the players and fans. It was great hearing the testimonies from many of the professionals about their faith in Christ and how he has used them for his glory in their lives and on the course. But even better, I loved that Blake was there to hear their stories with me. That morning made an indelible impact on his faith and life.

Later that afternoon, Blake and I were asked to help teach a junior golf clinic at a local club, and I got a chance to see him interacting with another young man—a boy who was termi-

> I TRY TO LEARN FROM EVERYONE. I LOOK AT THEIR STRENGTHS AND ASK MYSELF, "WHAT CAN I DO BETTER."
>
> ANNIKA SORENSTAM

nally ill and had been brought to Augusta by the Make-a-Wish Foundation to watch the tournament. I had to fight back the tears as I watched Blake work with this young man, spending most of the afternoon helping him with his swing and making him feel special. Seeing my young son pass on his passion to this little boy and mentor him on the course brought more joy to my heart than I can possibly put into words.

WHERE'S YOUR MAN?

I have the greatest respect for the Navigator Ministry, headquartered in Colorado Springs, Colorado. More than any organization that I'm aware of, they have done outstanding work around the globe to bring people to Christ and then to mentor them in their new faith.

The Navigators bring to the body of Christ a unique philosophy of spiritual growth through discipleship. Dawson Trotman, the founder of this worldwide organization, was a firm believer not only in leading people to salvation but in working with them afterward, mentoring them and teaching them how to share their faith with others. He called it "spiritual multiplication"—a term that is still used to embody the ministry's philosophy and role within God's earthly kingdom.

> I'M JUST A PLOWHAND FROM ARKANSAS, BUT I HAVE LEARNED HOW TO HOLD A TEAM TOGETHER—HOW TO LIFT SOME MEN UP, HOW TO CALM OTHERS DOWN, UNTIL FINALLY THEY'VE GOT ONE HEARTBEAT TOGETHER AS A TEAM. . . . THAT'S ALL IT TAKES TO GET PEOPLE TO WIN.
>
> COACH "BEAR" BRYANT

The Navigator's philosophy is grounded in Dawson's understanding of 2 Timothy 2:2. In this verse, Paul is talking to Timothy, his spiritual son, and says to him, "And the things you have heard me say in the presence of many witnesses entrust to reliable men who will also be qualified to teach others." This passage, Dawson explains, is a charge for Christians to sow into the lives of others, from generation to generation. Just as Paul mentored Timothy, he encourages him to mentor other believers, who will in turn pass their faith on to others. It's a simple principle, yet more effective than any other I've seen.

When meeting with other believing men, Dawson was well known for his habit of turning to another man and asking, "Where's your man?" What he meant by that phrase was, "Who are you mentoring right now in your life?" He was a firm believer that every Christian should have at all times at least one person they are working with and discipling in the faith. More than that, he believed that every believer should also have a mentor—someone they could look to for guidance and direction.

Dawson used to say, "Somewhere in the body of Christ there is a Paul waiting to mentor you, and a Timothy waiting to be mentored by you." Today the Navigators still hold firmly to that credo.

But mentoring implies more than just sharing your faith with someone or guiding a brother into truth. In 2 Timothy 3:10–11, Paul says to his young apprentice, "You, however, know all about my teaching, my way of life, my purpose, faith, patience, love, endurance, persecutions, sufferings—what kind of things happened to me in Antioch, Iconium and Lystra, the persecutions I endured. Yet the Lord rescued me from all of them."

Paul did much more than teach Timothy; he ushered Timothy deep inside his world, letting him know "all about" his life and faith. Timothy witnessed Paul's life from inside the ropes. He was given free access to Paul's successes and failures, to his purpose and sufferings and faith—to his "way of life." No secrets and no questions were considered off limits. Paul led Timothy into his heart and mind while working to disciple him.

Jesus said to his disciples, "Go and make disciples of all nations" (Matt. 28:19). In effect, he was asking them, "Where's your man?"

That's a good question for you and me, as well.

36

KEEP THE GAME IN
PERSPECTIVE

One of the hardest working golfers I ever knew was Bob Unger. I met Bob and his wife, Jenny, in the early 70s while we were both struggling through mini-tours, trying to qualify for the tour. They were great people, but neither of them had a relationship with the Lord.

Bob and Jenny lived and breathed golf. They owned a motor home and would park it on the edge of the parking lots at the tournament courses, and that's where they would live until the next event. They had very few interests outside of Bob's golf career and were intent on remaining focused only on his game.

Bob practiced harder and longer than any player I'd ever met. And he had an amazing talent for the game. He was both skilled and determined, and he had everything needed to become a tour professional. All the pros were sure he was going to make it, because he had done so well on the mini-tours.

Debbie and I got to know Bob and Jenny both on and off the course. They were completely wrapped up in the game of golf, intent on seeing that nothing deterred Bob from focusing on his game and gaining his card.

Then, the night before the first round of qualifying school at Perdido Bay Country Club in Pensacola, Florida, Debbie and I took the opportunity to share our faith with Bob and tell him about Jesus. I could tell by his eyes he was coming to understand the truth of God's message, but something was holding him back. I knew that if I could ever get Bob to accept Jesus as his Savior, he

> **GOLF IS NOT MY GOD. GOLF IS A GAME. JESUS CHRIST IS MY GOD.**
>
> PAUL AZINGER

would be an amazing witness for Christ. He didn't do anything halfway—it wasn't in his makeup. Bob was a passionate person who threw himself headlong into everything he did. Finally toward the end of the evening, Bob turned to me and said, "I think I need to accept Jesus. Would you pray with me?"

I was overjoyed and prayed with Bob as he accepted Jesus as his Lord.

That night Bob told Jenny about his decision, and she was not a happy camper. The first thought that popped into her mind was that this was going to throw off his game. She knew her husband too well to think he could focus on his playing with this new faith burning in his heart. "Couldn't you just wait two weeks?" she asked him. "Wait until after qualifying school, then you can become a Christian."

But she was too late. Bob had made his decision and there was no turning back. He convinced Jenny to pray with him that night and ask Jesus into her life as well, and she agreed to do it. She admitted later, however, that she had only been trying to please Bob. Throughout his prayer, she continued to worry about what this was going to do to his game.

Qualifying school that year consisted of eight grueling rounds of golf on two different courses—beginning at Pensacola and finishing over six hundred miles away at Myrtle Beach. Bob started at Perdido

Country Club with a strong opening round of 69 and a decent second day of 71, but his game started going downhill from there. The longer he played, the harder he found it to keep his mind in his game instead of on his new decision to follow Christ. And the greater his zeal for the Lord grew, the more his game deteriorated. He shot a 75 and a 77 on the next two days of qualifying, which pushed him far back in the pack—around sixtieth place.

> WE WILL ALL GRIP SOMETHING, AND WE WILL ALL BE GRIPPED BY SOMETHING OR SOMEONE. SO MY QUESTION TO YOU IS, "DO YOU HAVE A GRIP ON YOUR LIFE?" YOU MAY HAVE A CONTROLLED BACKSWING, BUT DO YOU HAVE CONTROL DOWN INSIDE? YOUR ANSWER IS CRITICAL TO YOUR SUCCESS IN THE GAME OF LIFE.
>
> BILLY GRAHAM

Bob knew he was down, but not yet out. He and Jenny quickly packed for the long ten-hour drive to Myrtle Beach. Then just as they started out of the parking lot in their large motor home, Jenny began to cry and unload on him. "You're such a good player," she told him, "and you've worked so hard for this. You've got everything you need to make it onto the tour; we both know that. But now you've just lost your heart for the game. I knew this would happen when you decided to become a Christian!"

As Jenny sat crying uncontrollably, Bob pulled the motor home over to the side of the road and said to her, "You're right. I'm a nervous wreck. And I can't seem to focus like I should. But I didn't ask Jesus into my life for nothing. I'm going to pray right now and put it in his hands. If he wants me to make it, he's got to give me the power. If not, I'll do whatever he wants me to do—I'll work at a hamburger stand if that's what he wants. I'll quit golf if he doesn't want me to play. But I want that to be his decision."

Then Bob took Jenny by the hand and said a simple prayer, laying his game and his future at the feet of Jesus. Afterward he looked at Jenny and said, "Okay, now we've given it to the Lord and we don't have to worry about it anymore. When I'm playing I want you to watch me. Whether I play well or mess up, I'm going to look over at you and point my finger in the air. That means 'one way.' Whatever happens, Jesus is in control."

Jenny wasn't sure what to think of Bob's new philosophy of golf, but she was willing to go along with anything that might help him get his mind back into his game. During the last four rounds of qualification, Bob's game came around. He was playing some of the best golf of his life. In spite of some of the worst weather of the year, Bob shot par golf all the way through to finally gain his PGA card. He ended up with the second lowest score during the last four rounds of playing, just behind Ben Crenshaw.

Throughout the rounds Bob did exactly what he told Jenny he would do. He put his trust in Jesus, and with each shot, he looked over at her and pointed his finger in the air. "One way." Players who were paired with him during those rounds couldn't believe Bob's commitment to staying focused on the Lord. They later testified that before each shot Bob would bow his head and say a simple prayer, then look over at Jenny and lift his finger into the air with a smile.

Some months later Bob was able to lead Jenny into a deep and personal relationship with Jesus. Bob had a great two-year career on the PGA tour, but it paled in comparison to his new faith in Jesus. I've long since lost count of the number of people he and Jenny led to the Lord through his days on tour. They were a shining example of true faith on the professional golf circuit.

Today Bob is a full-time pastor. He and Jenny work with an exciting church just outside of Colorado Springs, Colorado. Since the day that they each gave their hearts to Christ, they have never waned from keeping Jesus at the center of their lives.

THE TRUE BEAUTY OF THE GAME

I recently had the chance to have dinner with Bob and Jenny and later to visit with them in their church home. I asked Bob if he gets to play much golf these days. "I play a few times a year," he said, "usually with some guys from our church. And I still love it. I wish I could play more often, but the ministry keeps me pretty busy."

As great as golf is to play, the true genius of the game is the way it brings so many lives together and builds lifelong friendships in the process. I've forgotten many of the games and scores and great shots of my career, but I'll always remember the people I met along the way. God has used this great game to bring people into my life that I probably never would have met or developed friendships with otherwise, and for that I am eternally grateful.

> **AND IF YOU PLAY GOLF, YOU'RE MY FRIEND.**
>
> HARVEY PENICK

Though I wish I could see my friends more often, it's comforting to know that someday, sooner than we may think, we'll all meet again for one last round on the great nineteenth hole in the sky. I'll be there with my Gator bag and my 1953 Wilson sand wedge, with Joe the Pro carrying my clubs. As always, he'll probably be bragging about the Gators and cutting up with Bob and Jenny and all the rest of the gang. And I'll still be telling the gallery about my incredible tee shot on the sixteenth hole at Cypress Point for a tap-in birdie.

Make sure you're there to join us.

Until then, stay in his grip, and I'll see you at the tee!

PERSONALITIES QUOTED

Louie Anderson, comedian and best-selling author. Quote taken from his book *Dear Dad*.

Tommy Armour, professional golfer. Winner of the 1990 Phoenix Open and the 1993 Mexican Open.

Paul Azinger, professional golfer. Winner of twelve PGA tournaments and two international events. Named 1993 PGA Champion. Cocaptain of the 1994 President's Cup competition.

John E. Baxter, golf writer from the early 1920's. Author of *Locker Room Ballads*.

Henry Beard, author of numerous books, including *Golf Your Way*.

Patty Berg, professional golfer. Founding member of the LPGA Tour. Winner of 57 tournaments, including fifteen majors. Three-time AP Female Athlete of the Year (1938, 1943, 1955). Inducted into the Sports Hall of Fame.

Coach "Bear" Bryant, legendary head football coach of the University of Alabama, 1958–1982.

Percy Boomer, golf teacher in the 1940s and 1950s. Author of *On Learning Golf*.

Jack Burke Sr., professional golfer in the early 1900s. 1941 PGA Seniors Champion. Inventor of the all-weather grip.

Billy Casper, professional golfer. Winner of fifty-one PGA tour events, including the Masters and two U.S. Opens. Represented the U.S. in eight Ryder Cup competitions, winning more points than any other American player (23.5). PGA Player of the Year in 1966 and 1970.

Oswald Chambers, best-selling author of *My Utmost for His Highest*.

Fred Couples, professional golfer. Winner of fourteen tournaments, including 1992 Masters. PGA Player of the Year in 1991 and 1992.

Dave Dravecky, former all-star pitcher for the San Francisco Giants, best-selling author, and lecturer. Founder of Outreach of Hope Ministries.

Pete Dye, former president of the USGA and former commissioner of the PGA. Builder and architect of some of the greatest golf courses around the globe, including Crooked Stick in Carmel, Indiana; TPC at Sawgrass, in Ponte Vedra, Florida; and Old Marsh in West Palm Beach, Florida.

Dow Finsterwald, professional golfer in the 1950s. Winner of twelve PGA tournaments, including the 1958 PGA Championship. Winner of the Vardon Trophy in 1957 and PGA Player of the Year in 1958.

Raymond Floyd, professional golfer. Winner of twenty-two PGA tournaments, fourteen Senior PGA tournaments, and over twenty-six international events.

Arnie Frankel, golf instructor with Frankel Golf Academy.

John Freeman, author of numerous books, including *Tee-Ology: Eighteen Inspirational Lessons for Golfers*.

Doug Ford, professional golfer in the 1950s. Winner of twenty-seven tournaments.

Billy Graham, evangelist and best-selling author. Founder of the Billy Graham Evangelistic Association.

Walter Hagen, professional golfer from the early 1900s. World's first full-time tournament professional. Winner of over forty PGA tournaments, including eleven major championships. Four-time winner of the British Open and six-time captain of the U.S. Ryder Cup team.

Ben Hogan, professional golfer. Winner of sixty-three PGA tour events, including nine major championships, two Masters, four U.S. Opens, and one British Open. Four-time PGA Player of the Year, three-time winner of the Vardon Trophy, and three-time captain of the U.S. Ryder Cup team. Leading money winner five times.

Arnold Haultain, author. Excerpts taken from his book *The Mystery of Golf.*

Ken Hubbard, American humorist, 1868–1930.

Hale Irwin, professional golfer. Winner of nineteen PGA tournaments, including three U.S. Opens and two Memorials. Represented the U.S. in five Ryder Cup competitions.

John Jacobs, professional golfer in the early 1900s. Winner of the Dutch Open and the South African Match Play Championship. Best known as a pioneer architect of European golf courses. Also a writer, commentator, and coach.

Jerry B. Jenkins, best-selling author. Has written over 140 books, including the best-selling *Left Behind* fiction series.

Bobby Jones, professional golfer in the early 1900s. Winner of four U.S. Opens, five U.S. Amateurs, and three British Opens. Played in six Walker Cup events. Won golf's Grand Slam, 1930.

Ernest Jones, golf instructor in the 1940s. Author of *Swing the Clubhead.*

Andra Kirkaldy, professional golfer from St. Andrews in the early 1900s. Author of *Fifty Years of Golf: My Memories.*

Joe Kirkwood, famous trick-shot artist in the early 1900s. Winner of several tournaments, including four consecutive events in 1929.

Tom Kite, professional golfer. Winner of nineteen PGA tournaments, three Senior PGA tournaments, and over eight international events.

Greg Laurie, evangelist and author.

Steven Lawson, author and pastor of Dauphin Way Baptist Church in Mobile, Alabama.

Tom Lehman, professional golfer. Winner of five PGA tournaments, four Buy.com Hogan tournaments, and two international events.

Tony Lema, professional golfer. Known as "Champagne Tony," for his tradition of passing out champagne to the press at tournaments. Winner of several tournaments, including the British Open. Killed in a plane crash in 1966.

Nancy Lopez, professional golfer. Winner of forty-three tournaments, including four major championships.

Davis Love III, professional golfer. Winner of ten PGA tournaments, including the 1992 Players Championship. Represented the U.S. in two Ryder Cup competitions and two President's Cup events. Winner of four consecutive World Cup competitions.

Max Lucado, best-selling author of over twenty books, including *No Wonder They Call Him the Savior* and *God Came Near*. Minister of Oak Hills Church in San Antonio, Texas.

Meg Mallon, professional golfer. Winner of eight LPGA tournaments, including two major events. Played in four Solheim Cup events.

Brennon Manning, best-selling author of *The Ragamuffin Gospel* and *Ruthless Trust*.

Byron Nelson, professional golfer. Winner of fifty-two PGA tournaments. Holds the record for the most wins in one calendar year (18) and the most consecutive wins (11)—both in 1945—and also for the most consecutive finishes in the money (113).

Jack Nicklaus, professional golfer. Named Player of the Century. Winner of seventy-one tour events, including twenty major championships, as well as five Senior PGA tournaments, including the 1991 Senior Open. Represented the U.S. in eight Ryder Cup competitions (twice as captain), six World Cup competitions, and two Walker Cup competitions.

Greg Norman, professional golfer. Winner of ninety tournaments worldwide, including two British Opens and eighteen PGA events. PGA Player of the Year in 1995 and three-time winner of the Vardon Trophy.

Mac O'Grady, professional golfer. Winner of two PGA tournaments.

David Owen, author of numerous books, including *The Chosen One: Tiger Woods and the Dilemma of Greatness* and *My Usual Game: Adventures in Golf.*

Arnold Palmer, professional golfer. Winner of ninety-two PGA events, including seven major championships, twelve Senior PGA tournaments, and nineteen international events. Holds the U.S. Amateur title. Represented the U.S. in six Ryder Cup competitions, seven World Cup competitions, and five Chrysler Cup events.

Harvey Penick, legendary golf instructor, author of *Harvey Penick's Little Red Book* and *And If You Play Golf, You're My Friend.*

Gary Player, professional golfer. Recognized as "the Black Knight" and "International Ambassador of Golf." Winner of 163 tournaments worldwide, including the Career Grand Slam. He has won nine majors on the Regular Tour and nine on the Senior Tour. The only player to win the Grand Slam on both tours. Also a record five World Match Play events, seven Australian Opens, thirteen South African Opens. Designer of over two hundred golf courses worldwide. Captain of the International Team for The President's Cup 2003.

E. M. Prain, journalist and entrepreneur in the early 1900s. Author of *Live Hands: A Key to Better Golf.*

Nick Price, professional golfer. Winner of sixteen PGA tournaments and twenty-four international events.

Grantland Rice, sports reporter and author.

Chi Chi Rodriguez, professional golfer. Winner of eight PGA tournaments and twenty Senior PGA tournaments.

Bob Rotella, author and Director of Sports Psychology at the University of Virginia. Consultant to numerous PGA, LPGA, and Senior PGA professionals. Writer and consultant for *Golf Digest*.

Paul Runyan, professional golfer in the early 1900s. Winner of twenty-eight PGA tour events, including two majors, two PGA Championships, and two Senior PGA events. Leading money winner in 1934.

Vivien Saunders, LPGA teacher from Great Britain. Author of *The Golfing Mind*.

Craig Shankland, sports writer. Excerpt taken from *Golf Illustrated*, May 1993.

Jim Sheard, author and lecturer. Cowriter with Wally Armstrong of *In His Grip, Finishing the Course,* and *Playing the Game*.

Sam Snead, professional golfer. Winner of eighty-one PGA tournaments, including three PGA Championships, one British Open, and three Masters. Represented the U.S. in eight Ryder Cup competitions and six World Cup competitions. Leading money winner three times. Four-time winner of the Vardon Trophy.

Annika Sorenstam, professional golfer. Winner of over thirty-one LPGA tournaments and nine LPGA awards, including Player of the Year four times. Won more LPGA tournaments than any other player in the 1900s (18). One of two players in LPGA history (with Karrie Webb) to earn $1 million in three separate seasons. Played in four Solheim Cup events.

Payne Stewart, professional golfer. Winner of eleven tour events, including the PGA Championship and the U.S. Open. Represented the U.S. in five Ryder Cup competitions. Killed in a plane crash in 1999.

Curtis Strange, professional golfer. Winner of seventeen tournaments, including two back-to-back U.S. Open titles. Leading money winner in 1985, 1987, and 1988. Represented the U.S. in four Ryder Cup competitions. PGA Player of the Year in 1988.

Bill Strausbaugh, former golf instructor at Columbia Country Club in Washington, D.C.

Louise Suggs, professional golfer. Winner of the U.S. Amateur, the British Amateur, and fifty LPGA tournaments. One of the "100 Heroes of American Golf."

J. H. Taylor, professional golfer in the early 1900s. Winner of five major championships, five British Opens, two French Opens, one German Open, and the 1908 British Match Play.

W. J. Thompson, golf writer from the early 1920s. Author of *Common Sense Golf.*

Bob Toski, golf instructor and part-time professional golfer. Author of numerous instructional books, including *The Complete Golfer,* with Jim Flick.

Harry Vardon, professional golfer in the early 1900s. Winner of sixty-two tournaments, including seven major championships, one U.S. Open, and six British Opens.

Ken Venturi, professional golfer. Winner of fourteen PGA tournaments, including the U.S. Open. PGA Player of the Year in 1964. Has served for twenty-five years as color commentator for CBS golf and is also a golf course design consultant.

Warren Wiersbe, author of numerous books, commentaries, and expositional studies of the Scriptures. Radio talk-show host, lecturer, and Bible scholar.

Gary Wiren, golf instructor and Master member of the PGA. Author of *The Teaching Manual* and over two hundred magazine articles and instructional booklets. Winner of numerous teaching awards, including PGA Teacher of the Year in 1987.

P. G. Wodehouse, English author of thirty-six golf novels and over six hundred short stories. One of England's most prolific golf writers in the 1930s and '40s.

Tiger Woods, professional golfer. Winner of over twenty-nine PGA tournaments and six international events. Has won all four majors consecutively—PGA's first Grand Slam. In 2000 posted one of the greatest years in the history of the game, setting or tying twenty-seven PGA tour records. In 1999 earned a tour record of over $6.6 million in earnings ($3 million more than David Duval, the nearest competitor).

Babe Didrikson Zaharias, professional athlete in the early 1900s. Won two gold medals in the 1932 Olympics (javelin and 80-meter hurdles), then went on to play professional baseball. Took up golf in 1935 and went on to win fifty-five professional and amateur events, including ten majors. Helped found LPGA in 1949. Six-time winner of AP Female Athlete of the Year Award and chosen in 1950 as AP Athlete of the Half-Century.

To contact Wally for information on golf clinics, seminars, and resources:

Wally Armstrong
PO Box 941911
Maitland, FL 32794
(407) 644-3398
www.wallyarmstrong.com
www.golfreach.org